WORKBOOKS

4th Grade

D1373684

Geography

Consultant Ira Wolfman

Educational Consultant Gary Werner

US Editor Margaret Parrish
Editor Arpita Nath
Art Editor Rashika Kachroo
Project Art Editor Tanvi Nathyal
Senior Art Editor Ann Cannings
Jacket Designer Dheeraj Arora
Cartography Team Deshpal Dabas, Rajesh Mishra
Cartography Manager Suresh Kumar
Managing Editor Soma B. Chowdhury
Art Director Martin Wilson
DTP Designer Dheeraj Singh
Producer, Pre-Production Nadine King
Producer Priscilla Reby

First American Edition, 2016
Published in the United States by DK Publishing
1450 Broadway, Suite 801, New York, NY 10018

Copyright © 2016 Dorling Kindersley Limited
DK, a Divison of Penguin Random House LLC
16 17 18 19 20 10 9 8 7 6 5
005–284613–Jan/2016

A catalog record for this book
is available from the Library of Congress.
ISBN: 978-1-4654-4423-3

DK books are available at special discounts when purchased
in bulk for sales promotions, premiums, fund-raising,
or educational use. For details, contact: DK Publishing Special
Markets, 1450 Broadway, Suite 801, New York, NY 10018
SpecialSales@dk.com

Printed and bound in Canada

All images © Dorling Kindersley Limited
For further information see: www.dkimages.com

A WORLD OF IDEAS:
SEE ALL THERE IS TO KNOW
www.dk.com

Contents

This chart lists all the topics
in the *book*.

★ What is Geography?

FACTS

Geography helps us understand more about the planet on which we live. Geography tells us about the natural world, such as continents, mountains, oceans, and rivers. It also makes us aware of things built by humans, such as cities, bridges, and tunnels.

How well do you know your planet? Look at the numbers on this map of the Earth and the names in the word box below. Write the name for each number. **Note:** The first one has been done for you.

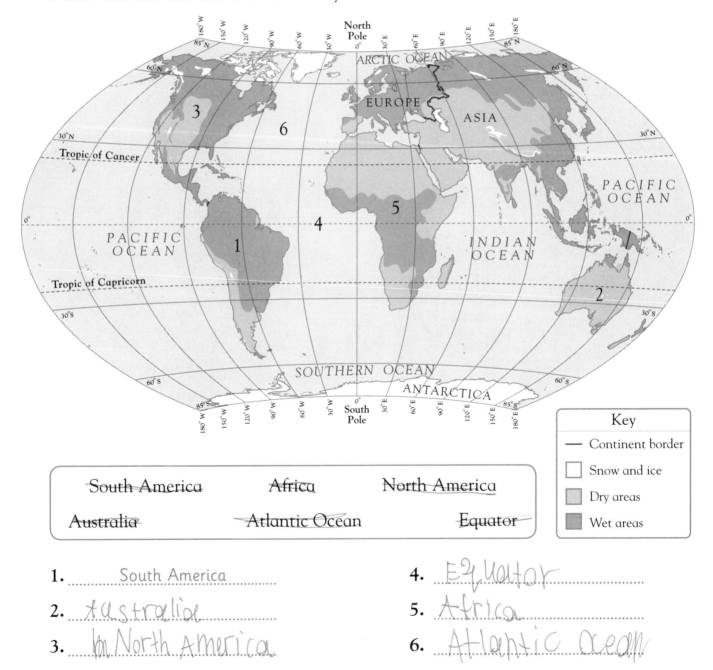

Word Box		
South America	Africa	North America
Australia	Atlantic Ocean	Equator

Key
— Continent border
☐ Snow and ice
▨ Dry areas
▨ Wet areas

1. _____South America_____

2. _____Australia_____

3. _____bn North America_____

4. _____E9 uaitor_____

5. _____Africa_____

6. _____Atlantic ocean_____

FACTS

The surface of the Earth is covered with landmasses, oceans, deserts, forests, and other natural features. Most of these have been here for millions of years, but things have changed over time. People have built cities and highways. Some forests have been cut down to make way for buildings. Storms, floods, or fire have also changed the way some places look.

Below are some landmarks from around the United States (US). Write **N** for a natural feature and **B** for something built by humans.

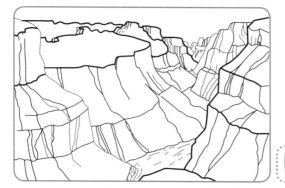

Grand Canyon, Arizona

Willis Tower, Illinois

Niagara Falls, New York

Pikes Peak, Colorado

Kennedy Space Center, Florida

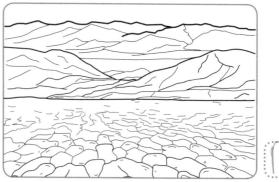

Death Valley, California

FACTS

Maps show where places are located. They explain where a place is in relation to other places. For example, a city map can help you locate a museum by showing that it is around the corner from a place you know, such as a library. City maps include street names and numbers.

Look at this map of Sacramento, California. Use the map to answer the questions below.

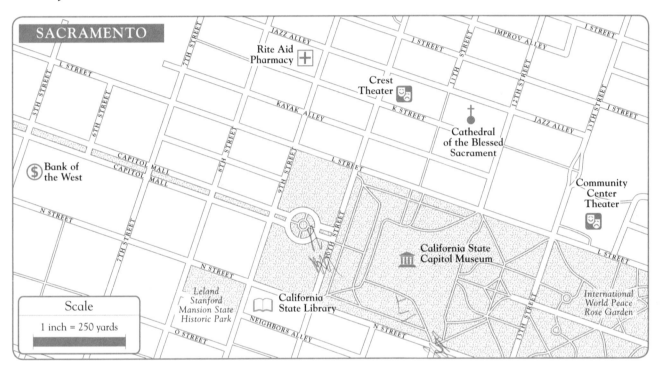

1. Which theater is closest to the pharmacy?

   crest theater

2. What building is east of the Leland Stanford Mansion Park?

   california state library

3. To reach the bank from the library, which street can you take?

   N Stb

4. What is the name of the garden close to the Community Center Theater?

   Rose garden

Key	
✝	Church
🏛	Museum
✚	Pharmacy
📖	Library
$	Bank
🎭	Theater
▨	Park/Garden

To use most maps, we need to know the four major directions—north, south, east, and west. Wherever we are on Earth, only one direction leads to the North Pole—north! South is exactly the opposite direction. The sun appears every morning in the east and disappears in the west. Knowing a map's compass directions shows which way you should go to reach a certain place.

Compass: A compass is an instrument with a needle that always points toward the North Pole. Compasses also show other directions.

Compass Rose: Most maps include a compass rose, which is a drawing of a compass. The compass rose helps users understand directions on maps.

Look at the map on the previous page. Use the compass rose to answer these questions.

1. Is the California State Capitol Museum northwest or northeast of the library?

   north east

2. If you head southeast from the pharmacy to go to the cathedral, which building will you pass?

   Crest theater

3. Name the street that lies south of the California State Library.

   Neighbors alley

4. Using compass directions, describe how you would go from the California State Library to the cathedral.

   north east

Maps show information using symbols. These symbols are markers that represent streets, parks, bodies of water, highways, and so on. In the map of a state, a star may stand for the capital city and solid dots may stand for the major cities. These symbols and their explanations are included in boxes called keys or legends.

Study this map of the US state of Florida, with its many symbols. Each number is pointing to a symbol. Use the key and write the correct word for each symbol.

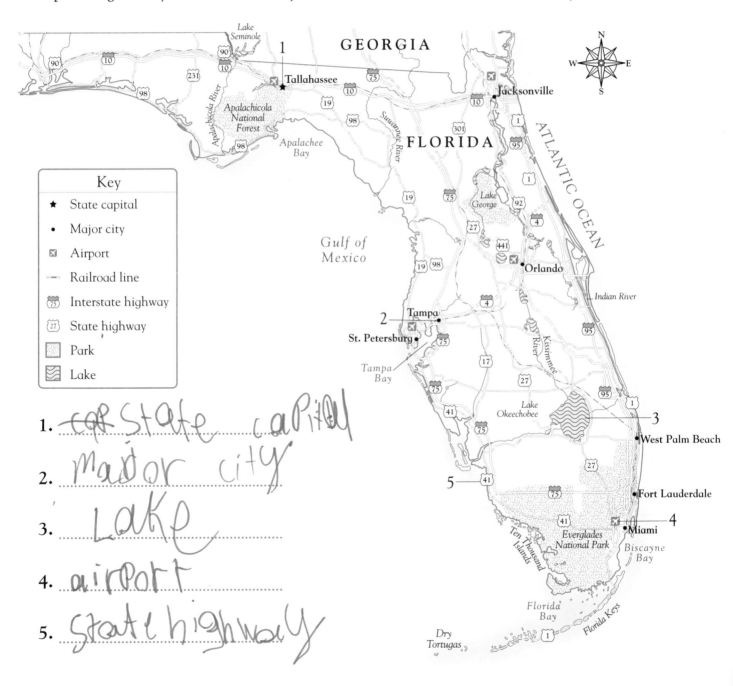

Key

★	State capital
•	Major city
✈	Airport
‑‑‑	Railroad line
75	Interstate highway
27	State highway
▦	Park
〰	Lake

1. ~~for~~ State capital

2. Major city

3. Lake

4. airport

5. State highway

Map Scale ★

FACTS

Every map is smaller than the place it shows. To make it possible to show big places on a map, mapmakers use a tool called scale. The scale is a line that tells us how much a certain distance on the map represents.

This map of the state of Tennessee shows its many cities. Use the scale above the map and a ruler to find answers to the questions. Then, circle the correct answers below.

Scale

1 inch = 75 miles

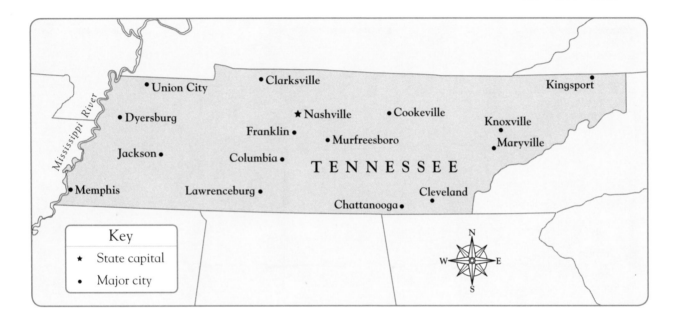

1. How far is Dyersburg from Maryville?

   a. 260 miles   **b.** 300 miles

2. Calculate the approximate distance between Nashville and Memphis.

   a. 188 miles   **b.** 200 miles

3. What is the approximate distance between Chattanooga and Cookeville?

   a. 75 miles   **b.** 85 miles

4. Which distance is longer?

   a. Memphis to Lawrenceburg   **b.** Franklin to Knoxville

Grids and City Maps

Cities can be complicated places with hundreds of streets. To help people find streets and buildings, maps include a grid and an index. A grid is a series of crisscrossing lines that divide the map into boxes. One side of the map is labeled with letters and the other side with numbers. You can find locations using the grid numbers, which are listed in the map's index.

The map below shows a part of the city of Philadelphia, Pennsylvania, and some of its landmarks. Use it to answer the questions below.

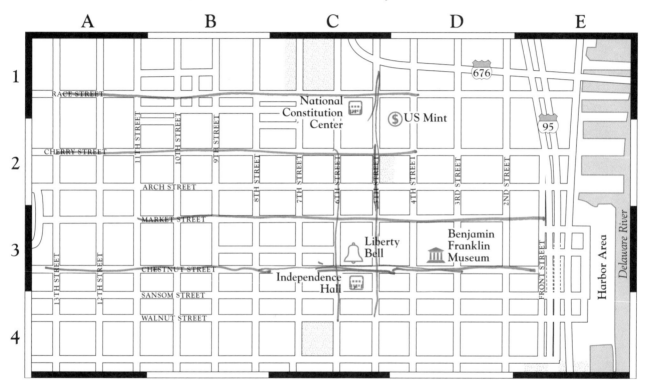

1. This building is between Race Street and Cherry Street, just west of 5th Street. What is its grid number and the name of the place?

   Building

2. Just south of Chestnut Street, between 5th and 6th streets, is a building where an important document was signed. What is its grid number and what is the name of the building?

   Intependence hall B3

3. In grid D3, between Market Street and Chestnut Street, there is a building named after a famous person. Name it.

Key	
95	Interstate highway
🏢	Building
🏛	Museum
🔔	Bell
$	Mint
▢	Park/Garden

Maps of Countries

More than 190 countries exist in the world today, and there is a map for each one. Country maps show us the shape of the country's borders, the names of its big cities, and the location of important natural features and landmarks built by humans.

This map shows Slovenia, a small country in southern Europe, surrounded by Italy, Austria, Hungary, and Croatia. Two million people live in Slovenia's cities and countryside. Use the map to circle the correct answers below.

1. Which neighboring country is closest to the Snežnik Castle?

   a. Italy   **b.** Croatia   **c.** Hungary

2. What is the capital city of Slovenia?

   a. Škofja Loka   **b.** Krvavec   **c.** Ljubljana

Key	
★	Country capital
●	Other city
■	Feature
〰	Lake

3. Which of these is a river in Slovenia?

   a. Krka   **b.** Bohinj   **c.** Jasna

★ Maps and Globes

Earth can be shown using flat maps and globes. Globes are shaped like the Earth, and they show the planet more accurately than flat maps. Although both are useful, maps are easier to carry. While flat maps are great for finding directions, globes are best for understanding how all the parts of our world make up one planet.

Look at the globe and the flat map below. Then read the statements below and check (✔) if each one is **true** or **false**.

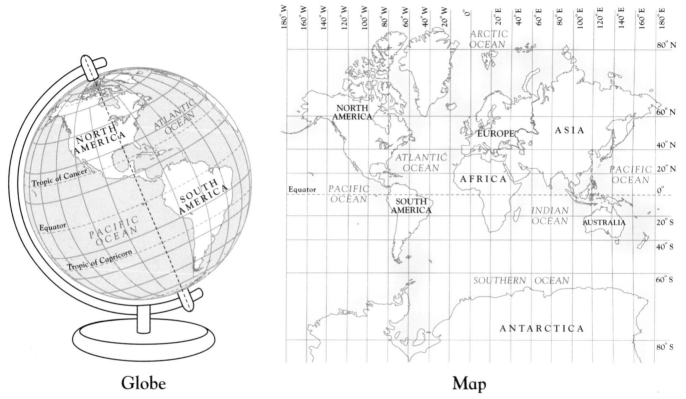

Globe   Map

Feature	True	False
Globes are better at showing the North and South poles.	✓	
Maps show Earth's shape better than globes.		✗
On a map, you can see everything on Earth at one glance.	✓	✗
Globes are easier to carry than maps.		✗
Globes are better at showing how Earth rotates.	✓	

FACTS

Maps and globes show the same Earth. It is, however, impossible to represent perfectly a round world on a flat map. Every world map shows something inaccurately. It could be the land's size or shape, or the distances between places. Mapmakers use different techniques, called projections, to show the curved surface of the Earth. Here are two of them:

Mercator Projection: This projection shows directions well. However, the places far from the equator are distorted and look too large.

Interrupted Projection: This projection presents the shapes and sizes of land accurately, but the distance and directions shown are not true or accurate.

Look at the Mercator and Interrupted map projections. Then read the statements and check (✓) if each one is **true** or **false**.

Mercator projection

Interrupted projection

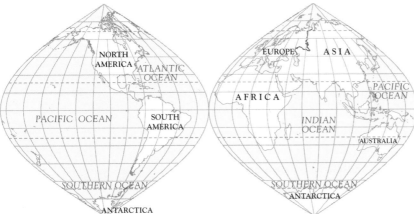

1. On the Interrupted map projection, Africa looks bigger than South America.

True ✓

False ☐

2. The Arctic and Antarctic regions are more accurate on the Mercator map.

True ☐

False ✓

3. The Interrupted projection is better at showing directions.

True ☐

False ✓

FACTS

Latitudes are imaginary lines that run horizontally across the Earth. They mark where something is in the north and south of our planet. They measure distance in degrees (°). The equator is latitude zero as it lies midway between the North and South poles. The North Pole is 90° north. The South Pole is 90° south. The latitudes in between are 1° to 89° north or south.

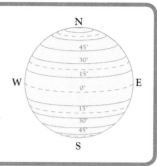

Iowa is a state located in the central United States. This map shows latitude lines of 41°, 42°, and 43° going east and west across Iowa. Use the map to answer the questions below.

Key	
★	State capital
•	Major city

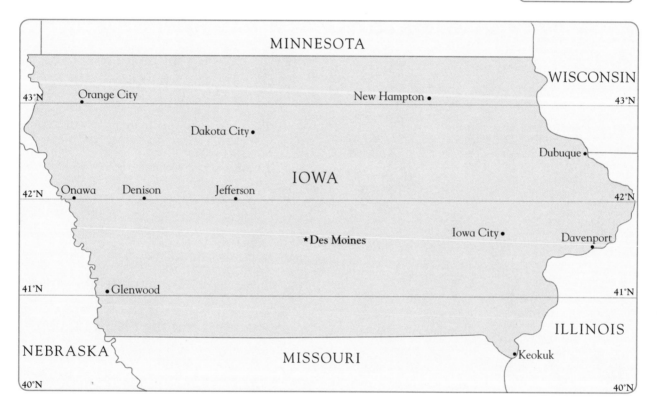

1. Which two lines of latitude does Iowa's capital, Des Moines, lie between?

....

2. On which latitude do Onawa, Denison, and Jefferson lie?

....

3. What is the only city on this map that sits exactly on the 43°N latitude line?

....

Longitude ★

Longitudes are imaginary lines that run from north to south across maps of the Earth. They come together at the North and South poles. The prime meridian is the 0° longitude, which passes through Greenwich, England. The Earth is divided into 360° of longitude—180° east of the prime meridian and 180° west.

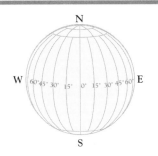

This map shows the state of Nebraska, which is just west of Iowa. Nebraska has longitudes ranging between 95° and 104° west. Use the map to answer the questions below.

Key	
★	State capital
•	Major city

SOUTH DAKOTA

104°W 103°W 102°W 101°W 100°W 99°W 98°W 97°W 96°W

MINNESOTA

WYOMING

• Harrison

• Valentine

• Bassett

IOWA

Mullen •

NEBRASKA

Columbus •

• Broken Bow

• Omaha

Sidney •

★ Lincoln

COLORADO

Beatrice •

• Benkelman

Pawnee City •

KANSAS

104°W 103°W 102°W 101°W 100°W 99°W 98°W 97°W 96°W

1. Sidney is a city in western Nebraska that sits exactly on a longitude. What is Sidney's longitude?

....

2. Omaha is Nebraska's most populous city. Which longitude lies just to its west?

....

3. Broken Bow is in the middle of the state. Which two longitude lines does it lie between?

....

4. Which city is located at longitude 101°W?

....

FACTS

The equator is the 0° latitude. It is an imaginary line that lies midway between the North Pole and the South Pole. It divides the Earth into the northern and southern hemispheres. Two other special latitude lines are the Tropic of Cancer, at 23.5° north, and the Tropic of Capricorn, at 23.5° south. Between these two lines are the regions called the tropics, which are the hottest areas on Earth.

This map of the world shows the special latitude lines. Use it to answer the questions below.

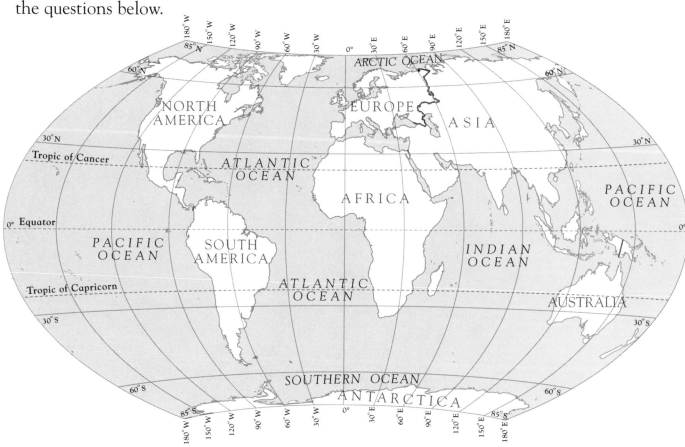

1. The Tropic of Capricorn passes through three continents. South America is one of them. Name the other two.

....

2. Two continents are not touched by any of those three latitude lines. Which are they?

....

3. Only one of the seven continents has all the three special latitude lines passing through it. Which continent is this?

....

4. Does the Tropic of Cancer pass through North America?

....

Hemisphere means "half of a sphere." Imaginary lines divide the Earth into four hemispheres. The equator, which is the 0° latitude, divides the Earth into the northern and southern hemispheres. The prime meridian, which is the 0° longitude, divides the Earth into the eastern and western hemispheres.

Look at these maps showing the four hemispheres. Read the statements below and check (✔) if each one is **true** or **false**.

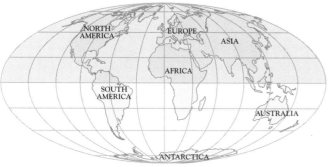

Northern hemisphere (N)

Western hemisphere (W)

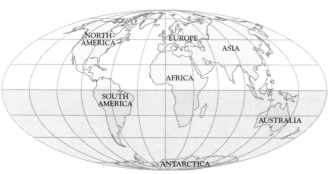

Southern hemisphere (S)

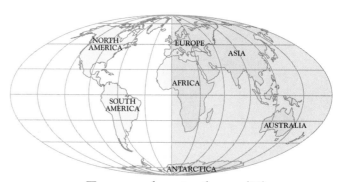

Eastern hemisphere (E)

1. Most of Earth's land can be found in the southern hemisphere.

True ☐   False ☐

2. Most of Europe is located in the western hemisphere.

True ☐   False ☐

3. Antarctica is located in all the four hemispheres.

True ☐   False ☐

4. No continent is located only in one hemisphere.

True ☐   False ☐

From space, Earth looks like a blue ball. This is because about 70 percent of its surface is water. The five salty oceans—the Pacific, Atlantic, Indian, Southern, and Arctic oceans—make up 96 percent of all water on Earth. Other bodies of water, such as freshwater lakes, ponds, and rivers, make up just four percent.

The oceans on Earth are actually one giant body of water that interrupts the continents. Study this map showing the oceans and answer the questions below.

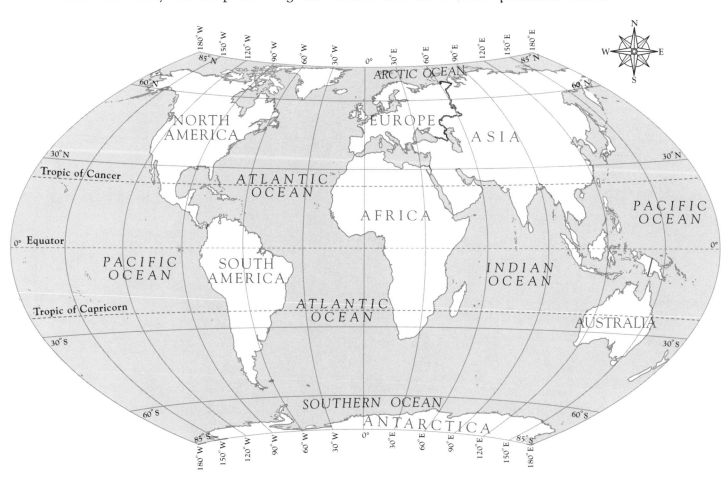

1. The .... Ocean is located north of Europe.

2. The .... Ocean touches the east coasts of North and South America.

3. Australia is bordered by the Indian Ocean to the west and the ....
Ocean to the east.

4. The body of water surrounding Antarctica is called the .... Ocean.

FACTS

Continents are the biggest masses of land on Earth. There are seven continents, with Asia being the largest. The other six, in order of size, are Africa, North America, South America, Antarctica, Europe, and Australia. Six of these are home to millions of people. The seventh, Antarctica, is a frozen continent and has a very small population of scientists living there to do research.

Study this map showing Earth's seven continents. Then answer the questions below.

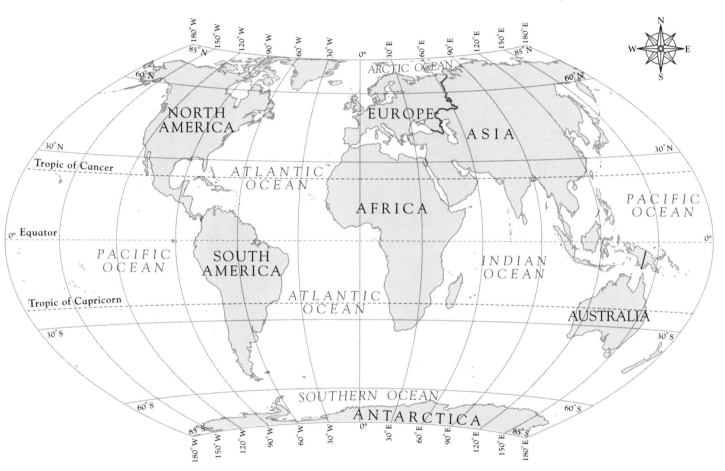

1. If you head east from Europe, you will reach this continent.

   ....

2. This continent is located just north of Africa and west of Asia.

   ....

3. The Atlantic, Pacific, and Arctic oceans surround this continent.

   ....

4. This continent is west of Africa and located mostly south of the equator.

   ....

★ North America

FACTS

North America is Earth's third-largest continent. Climate varies widely across North America. Areas near the Arctic Circle have a very cold climate, the middle regions are mostly temperate, and the southern areas are tropical. Around 600 million people live on this continent. There are more than 300 million people in the United States, 122 million in Mexico, and 35 million in Canada.

Study this map of North America showing its countries and some physical features. Then read the descriptions. On the map, write the letter next to the place that matches each description.

North America

A. This country is located south of the Sonoran Desert.

B. This is the continent's largest island. It borders on the Labrador Sea.

C. This country lies north of the Great Lakes.

D. This country is located just northwest of South America.

South America is Earth's fourth-largest continent. It is a land of contrasts. It is home to the snow-peaked Andes Mountains and the largest rain forest on Earth, the Amazon. South America begins just north of the equator but extends the farthest south of any continent. About 400 million people live in its 12 countries, including large ones, such as Brazil and Argentina, and smaller ones, such as Suriname and Ecuador.

Study this map of South America showing its 12 countries. Then using this map, write the name of the country that matches each description.

1. Landlocked countries do not have an ocean coastline. Name the two landlocked South American countries.

....

....

2. Of all these countries, which extends farthest to the east?

....

3. The equator runs across three countries. Name them.

....

....

FACTS

Africa is Earth's second-largest continent. It has more than 1 billion people spread across more than 50 countries. Africa is famous for its natural features, such as the Sahara—Earth's largest desert—and the Nile—Earth's longest river. Africa also has unusual wildlife, such as giraffes, elephants, and zebras.

Study this map showing some natural features of Africa. Read the statements below and check (✔) if each one is **true** or **false**.

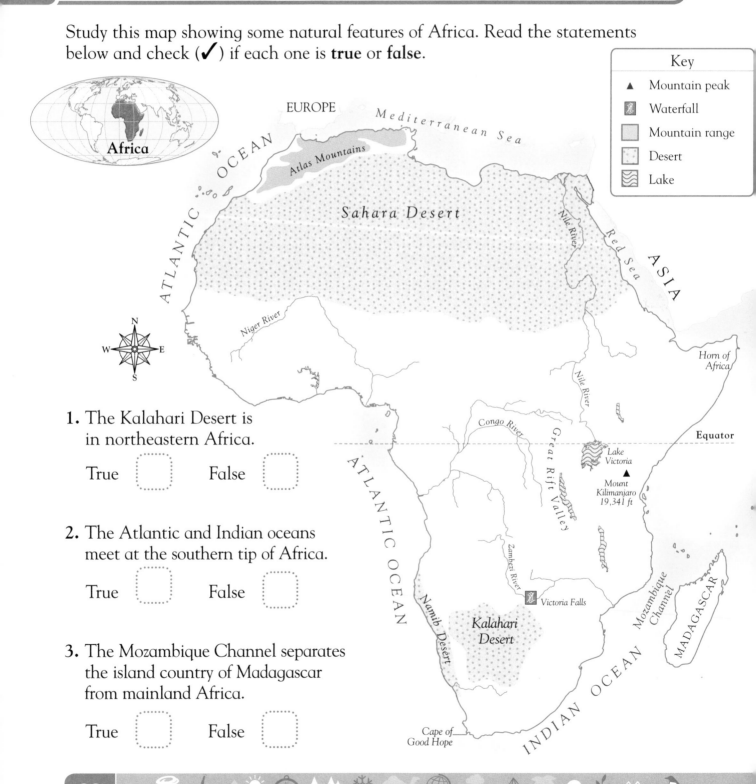

Key

▲ Mountain peak

Waterfall

Mountain range

Desert

Lake

1. The Kalahari Desert is in northeastern Africa.

True ☐   False ☐

2. The Atlantic and Indian oceans meet at the southern tip of Africa.

True ☐   False ☐

3. The Mozambique Channel separates the island country of Madagascar from mainland Africa.

True ☐   False ☐

Asia is Earth's largest continent. It stretches all the way from the cold grasslands of Siberia to the rain forests of Vietnam. Four billion people live in Asia. This is more than the number of people living on all the other continents combined. Asia also has Earth's tallest mountain chain, the Himalayas.

Unscramble the names of Asia's four most populated countries. Use this map of Asia to help you.

Scrambled Words	Country Name
Incha	
Niadi	
Napikast	
Gladabensh	

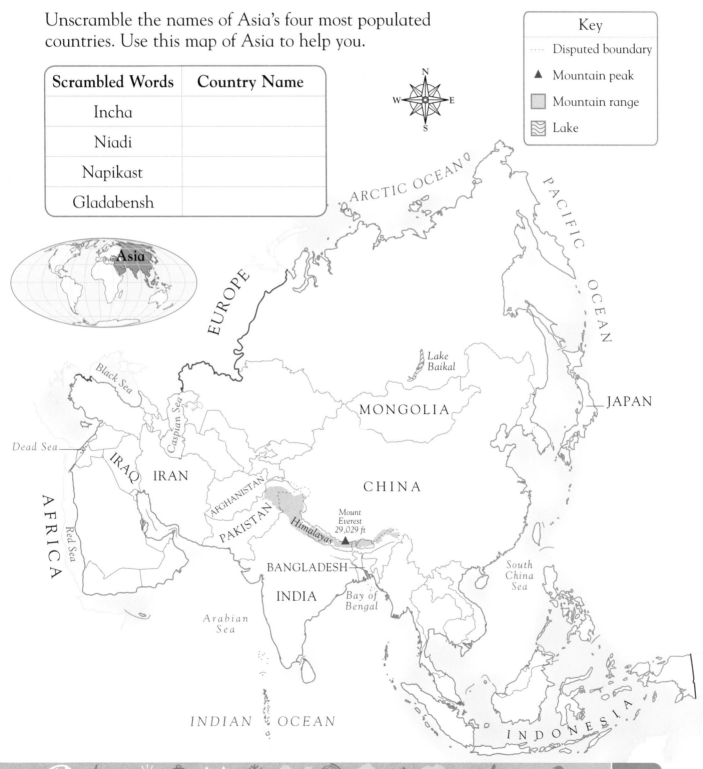

★ Australia

Australia is Earth's smallest continent. Although Australia is about the same size as the mainland United States, its population is less than that of California. The continent is famous for its wildlife, which includes kangaroos, koalas, and wallabies.

This map shows Australia and some nearby countries. Study the map and then circle the correct answers.

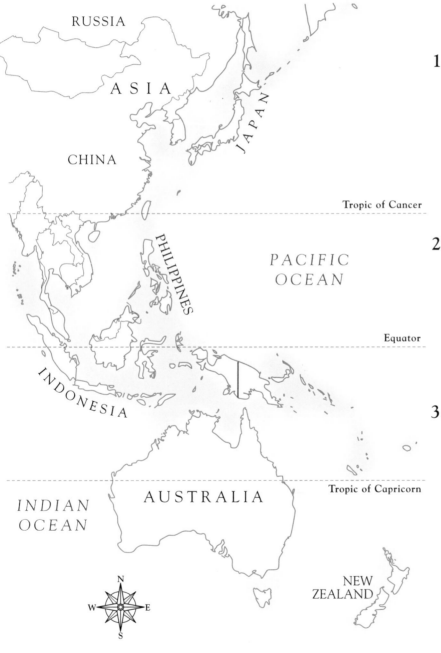

1. Which of these oceans surround Australia?
   a. Indian and Pacific oceans
   b. Atlantic and Indian oceans
   c. Arctic and Southern oceans

2. Which continent is closest to Australia?
   a. North America
   b. Asia
   c. South America

3. If you traveled southeast from Australia, which country would you reach?
   a. Indonesia
   b. Japan
   c. New Zealand

Europe is the second-smallest continent. It is connected to Earth's biggest continent, Asia. The Ural Mountains act as a natural border between the two. With 750 million residents, Europe is Earth's third-most populated continent.

This map shows four European capital cities. Imagine that you are traveling to each of them. Read the descriptions, and number the capital cities on the map in the order visited. **Note**: The first one has been done for you.

1. Your trip begins in Athens, the capital of Greece. Find the number 1.

2. You fly west across the Mediterranean Sea to Madrid, the capital of the southwestern country of Spain.

3. Next, you take a train to Berlin, the capital of the central European nation of Germany.

4. Finally, you drive east into the large neighboring country of Poland to its capital city, Warsaw.

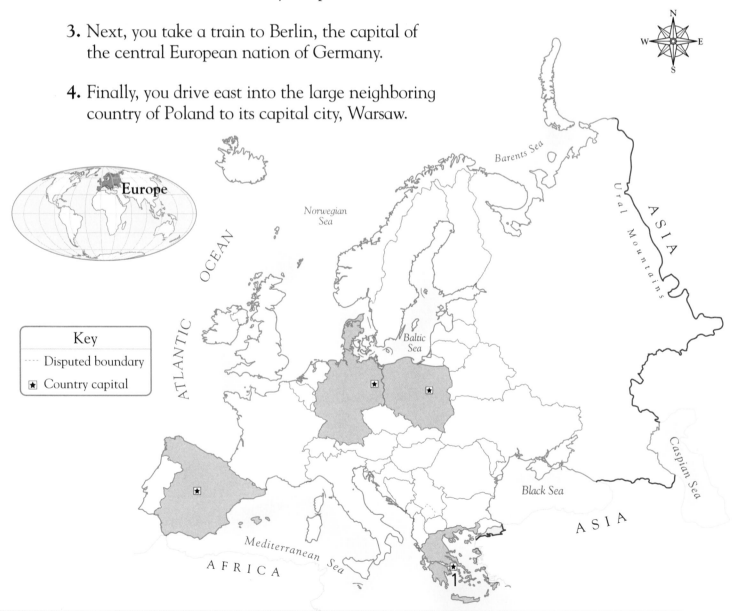

Antarctica is the coldest continent on Earth. In July 1983, it recorded Earth's lowest temperature, –128.6 °F (–89.2 °C)! Antarctica is located around the South Pole and has no permanent residents. The only people living there are scientists conducting research. However, lots of animals live in the waters nearby, including penguins, seals, dolphins, and whales.

This map shows the frozen continent, Antarctica. Find the letter on the map that matches each description. Then write the letter next to the appropriate description.

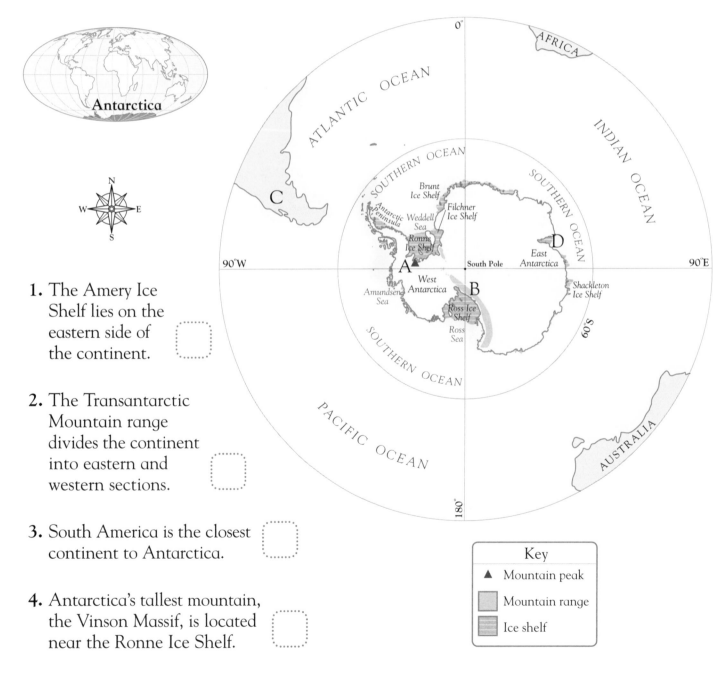

1. The Amery Ice Shelf lies on the eastern side of the continent.

2. The Transantarctic Mountain range divides the continent into eastern and western sections.

3. South America is the closest continent to Antarctica.

4. Antarctica's tallest mountain, the Vinson Massif, is located near the Ronne Ice Shelf.

Key

▲ Mountain peak

   Mountain range

   Ice shelf

Physical Features: Introduction

The Earth is covered with flat plains, high mountains, long rivers, deep lakes, evergreen forests, and sparse deserts. These natural features—landmasses, bodies of water, and types of vegetation—make up the planet we live on.

This map shows some of the natural features of North America. Study the map and then circle the correct answer.

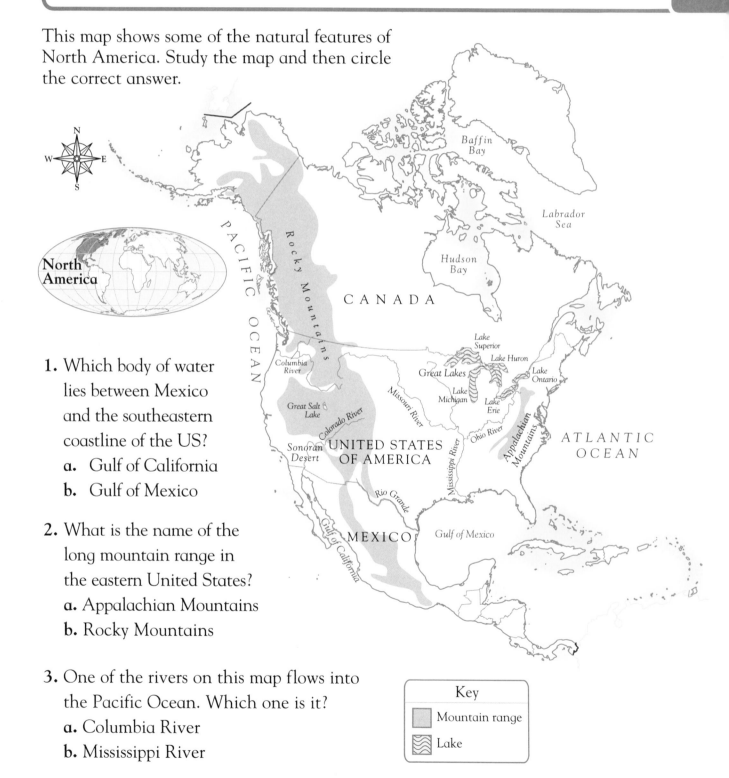

1. Which body of water lies between Mexico and the southeastern coastline of the US?
   a. Gulf of California
   b. Gulf of Mexico

2. What is the name of the long mountain range in the eastern United States?
   a. Appalachian Mountains
   b. Rocky Mountains

3. One of the rivers on this map flows into the Pacific Ocean. Which one is it?
   a. Columbia River
   b. Mississippi River

Key
Mountain range
Lake

Physical Features: Lakes

FACTS

Lakes are bodies of water that are surrounded by land on all sides. Most lakes are freshwater, though there are a few saltwater lakes. Many lakes were formed by the movement of giant sheets of ice, known as glaciers, many thousands of years ago. Unlike water in oceans and rivers, the water in lakes does not move much.

The state of Minnesota contains more than 12,000 lakes bigger than 10 acres. Look at this map of Minnesota showing some of its lakes. Then write their names to match the descriptions.

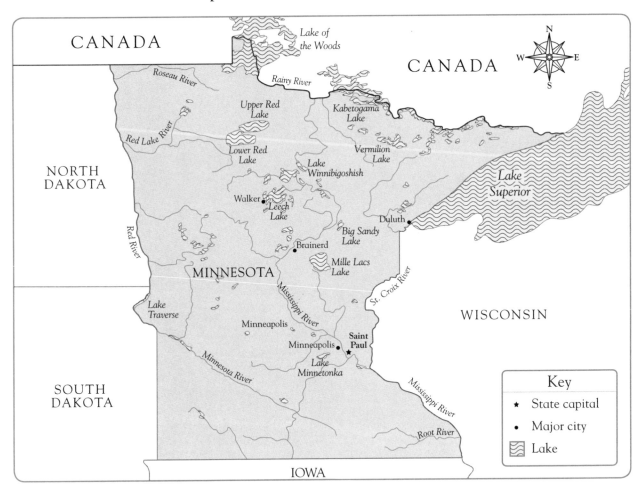

1. The Upper Red Lake is one of two twin lakes. Name the other one. ....

2. This is the largest lake on Minnesota's northern border. ....

3. Duluth is a port city located on this huge lake. ....

4. The city of Walker is on the western edge of this lake. ....

Physical Features: Rivers

Rivers are large flowing bodies of freshwater. They usually start in mountains or hills. Some are fed by rainwater or melting snow. From earliest times, rivers have provided people with drinking water and places to wash, catch fish, and travel by boat. All rivers flow into other, larger bodies of water, such as oceans, seas, lakes, and other rivers.

FACTS

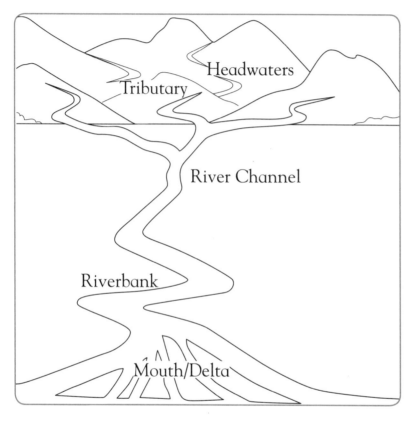

Headwater: Rivers start from here.

Tributary: A body of water that joins a river or flows into it.

River Channel: The path a river takes as it moves across the land.

Riverbank: The land alongside a river. When a river overflows its banks, floods happen.

Mouth or Delta: The area where a river ends by flowing into a larger body of water, usually an ocean or a lake.

Look at this picture showing a river. Then read the statements below and check (✔) if each one is **true** or **false**.

1. Rivers can be joined by other rivers.

   True ⬜   False ⬜

2. The mouth of a river is usually found in the mountains.

   True ⬜   False ⬜

3. Some rivers start as melting snow.

   True ⬜   False ⬜

4. Floods are caused by underground streams.

   True ⬜   False ⬜

Physical Features: Mountains

FACTS

Areas that are the high points on Earth's surface are called mountains. While some mountains slope up gradually, many others rise steeply. The Himalayas in Asia are the tallest mountain range on Earth. Mount Everest is the highest peak. It is more than 29,000 feet above sea level.

The highest mountain peaks on the seven continents are called "The Seven Summits." Look at the list below showing the heights of these peaks and the continents where they are found. Then find the mountains in the word search below.

Continent	Mountain	Height (in feet)
Asia	Everest	29,029
South America	Aconcagua	22,831
North America	Denali	20,310
Africa	Kilimanjaro	19,341
Europe	Elbrus	18,510
Antarctica	Vinson Massif	16,050
Australia	Kosciuszko	7,310

P	K	K	I	B	O	T	L	H	N	G	A	S	B	R
B	I	K	O	S	C	I	U	S	Z	K	O	U	R	V
W	L	O	E	L	Y	A	S	E	O	V	G	R	J	O
R	I	S	L	T	H	O	A	N	R	K	G	B	E	P
Q	M	C	B	C	I	M	B	D	V	E	P	L	V	D
C	A	I	R	D	P	O	D	E	N	A	L	I	E	Q
T	N	A	U	S	G	D	T	N	W	L	B	A	R	X
L	J	G	S	U	K	O	U	L	J	F	P	N	E	A
B	A	C	O	N	C	A	G	U	A	A	D	M	S	I
O	R	K	Y	E	L	N	I	R	C	M	R	T	T	M
I	O	V	I	N	S	O	N	M	A	S	S	I	F	X

Deserts are areas that receive less than 10 inches of rain in a year. Deserts can be hot and sandy or cold and frozen. Antarctica is a desert. These places are among the most difficult places to live because of the shortage of water and the harsh climate. However, some plants and animals do survive there.

The map and chart locate and describe the Sahara and Gobi deserts. Study them and then compare and contrast them, writing three similarities and three differences.
Note: The first one has been done for you.

Features	Gobi	Sahara
Type of desert	Cold	Hot
Location	Central Asia	North Africa
Size	At 500,000 square miles, it is Earth's fifth-largest desert.	At around 3.3 million square miles, it is Earth's largest desert.
Climate	Very cold winters; temperatures go as low as –40° F (–40 °C). Very hot summers; temperatures can rise above 100° F (37.7 °C).	Cool winters; temperature can go below 32° F (0 °C). In summers, this is one of the hottest places, where temperatures can rise over 134° F (56.6 °C).
Human population	Fewer than 3 people per square mile	Fewer than 1 person per square mile
Animal life	Bactrian (two-hump) camels, antelopes, gazelles, cattle, sheep, and goats	Dromedary (single-hump) camels, gerbils, and desert hedgehogs
Plant life	Some small bushes and desert-grass steppes	Grasses, shrubs, and palm trees only at oases

Similarities	Differences
1. Both deserts have very hot summers.	1. Both are home to different types of camel.

FACTS

Rain forests are dense, damp, tree-filled regions. Although they cover only two percent of the Earth's surface, about half of Earth's animal and plant species live in rain forests. Rain forest trees help humans by producing a huge amount of the oxygen we breathe in and absorbing carbon dioxide we breathe out. Earth's rain forests are endangered, so it is important that we find ways to protect them.

This map shows where some of the world's most important rain forests are located. Read each description, look at the map and then write the answers.

1. This rain forest is on a large island off the southeast coast of Africa. It is home to some very unusual animals, including the aye-aye, lemur, and half of the world's breeds of chameleon.

   ....

2. The equator runs through this rain forest in mainland Africa. This rain forest is around the Congo River. One famous animal of this huge rain forest is the mountain gorilla, which is now endangered.

   ....

3. This is the world's largest rain forest. It is mostly in Brazil but crosses many other South American countries. It contains one out of every five species of bird in the world! It is named after the river that runs through it.

   ....

Physical Features: Landforms

Land on Earth takes many forms. There are mountains and valleys, plateaus and canyons. The shape land takes affects the area's climate and its plant and animal life. These landforms were created over millions of years by natural forces.

Canyon, **peninsula**, **plateau**, and **valley** are types of landform. Look at the pictures and their descriptions. Then write the correct name of each landform on the dotted line.

This is a very deep, narrow area that is usually found between steep cliffs. It was carved out by a river.

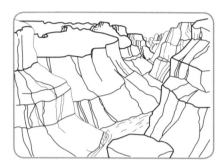

....

This is a body of land surrounded by water on three sides. It is attached at some point to another landform.

....

This is a landform that rises above its surroundings. It has a broad, flat area at its highest point.

....

This is a long, broad area of land lower than its surroundings. It may have been formed by a glacier or river.

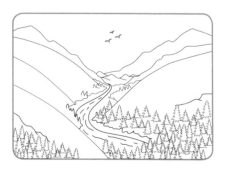

....

Maps help us get from one place to another, but that is just one of their uses. Maps show various kinds of information. Informational maps use pictures, symbols, and colors to show facts. For example, a map can show the changes in a region over 100 years.

This map shows the areas where the ruby-throated and rufous hummingbirds can be found on Earth. Study the map and then circle the correct answers.

North America

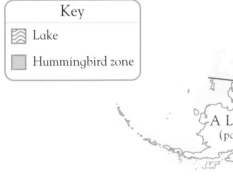

Key

⧉ Lake

▨ Hummingbird zone

1. Which part of North America does not have the ruby-throated and rufous hummingbirds?
   a. Mexico
   b. Greenland

2. Out of the following, which region has hummingbirds in all parts of it?
   a. the western region of the United States
   b. the eastern region of the United States

3. These hummingbirds are found in all of which area?
   a. Central America
   b. The United States

Types of Map: Political Maps

FACTS

A political map shows countries, states, cities, or territories. These maps show the government boundaries of these areas and display clearly where these regions begin and end. The boundary decisions are made by governments of countries. Since the word "politics" means "related to government," these maps are called political maps.

Look at this political map of Central America, the tropical region of North America, south of Mexico. Use the map to answer the questions below.

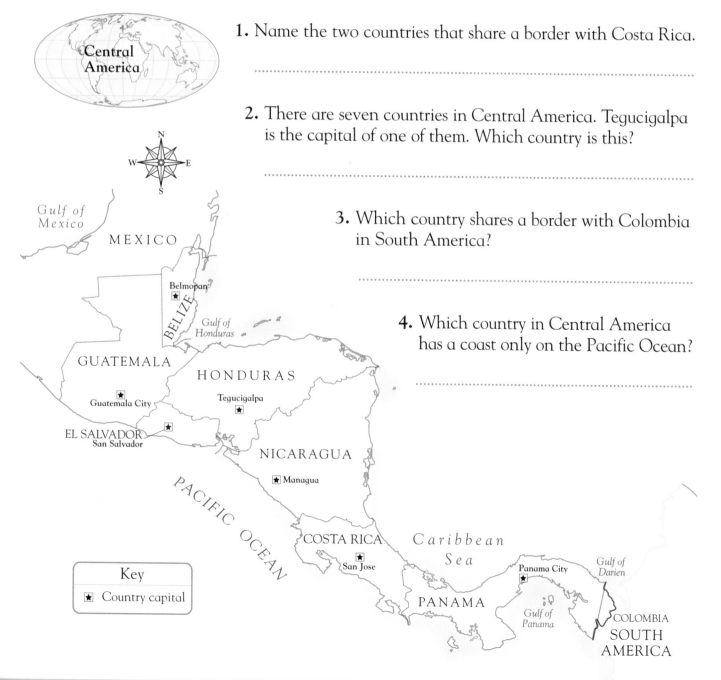

1. Name the two countries that share a border with Costa Rica.

....

2. There are seven countries in Central America. Tegucigalpa is the capital of one of them. Which country is this?

....

3. Which country shares a border with Colombia in South America?

....

4. Which country in Central America has a coast only on the Pacific Ocean?

....

FACTS:

Physical maps show the natural features of the Earth. These features include mountains, valleys, plains, rivers, lakes, and other areas of the natural world. Physical maps can show how mountainous or flat an area is. Information from them can be helpful for anyone who wants to farm, live, or build in that area.

Study this physical map of Europe. Then answer the questions.

1. Located north of the Carpathian Mountains, the country of .... does not have a major mountain range.

2. .... is a very small country located in the Pyrenees Mountains between Spain and France.

3. The long, narrow country of .... has a long coast on the Mediterranean Sea and a mountain range.

Key

- - - - Disputed boundary

〰 Lake

▨ Mountain range

Europe

Barents Sea

Kola Peninsula

Norwegian Sea

Ural Mountains

ASIA

North European Plain

ATLANTIC OCEAN

North Sea

Western Dvina River

Baltic Sea

Thames River

English Channel

Elbe River

Rhine River

POLAND

Vistula River

Volga River

Loire River

Seine River

Dnieper River

Bay of Biscay

FRANCE

Alps

Danube River

Carpathian Mountains

Don River

Caucasus Mountains

Caspian Sea

SPAIN

Pyrenees

ANDORRA

Po River

Apennine Mountains

ITALY

Balkan Mountains

Black Sea

Tagus River

Mediterranean Sea

ASIA

AFRICA

Road maps show the locations of cities and the roads that connect there. These maps show the names or numbers of highways in an area. Today, some people have electronic maps that use Global Positioning Systems or GPS, which give information about traffic on the roads, roads under construction, and even show alternate routes to the destination.

Key

★ State capital

• City

95 Interstate highway

40 State highway

1 Highway

Imagine that you are driving from Middletown, a small city in northern Delaware, to visit friends who reside in towns in southern Delaware. Read the descriptions below and decide which roads you will need to take to these cities.

1. You start at Middletown and your first stop is the town of Smyrna. You will head south on Highway 896 and join a state highway that will take you right up to Smyrna. Name the state highway that you will take.

   ....

2. After a day's stop at Smyrna, you travel to Frederica. After you pass Dover, you have to switch to another road. Which highway is it?

   ....

3. Dagsboro is your last stop and you will go via Milford. What state highway will take you to your final destination?

   ....

FACTS

Population maps show how many people live in an area. For such maps, country or state governments conduct a census, or a headcount, of the population. The census may also provide information about peoples' ages, professions, or backgrounds.

Study this map showing the population change in the US between 1900 and 2000. Read the statements below and check (✔) if each one is **true** or **false**.

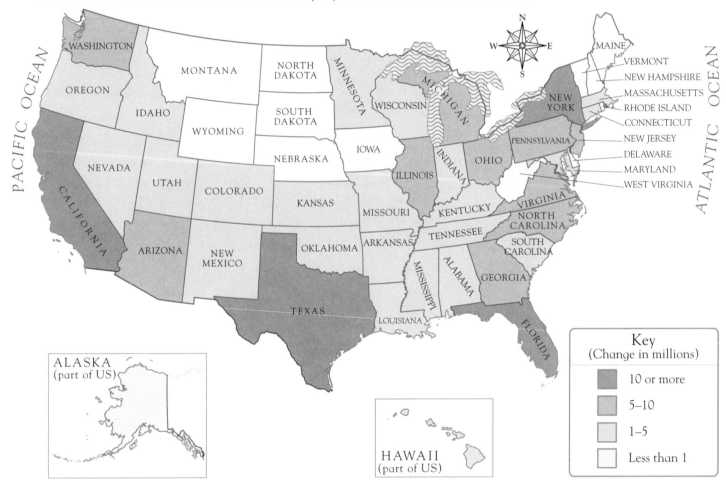

Key
(Change in millions)

- 10 or more
- 5–10
- 1–5
- Less than 1

ALASKA (part of US)

HAWAII (part of US)

1. In four states, the population increased by more than 10 million.

True ☐   False ☐

2. South Dakota's population grew more than South Carolina's.

True ☐   False ☐

3. Kansas gained more than 1 million people over the period of 100 years.

True ☐   False ☐

4. This map does not reveal the exact population of any state in the US.

True ☐   False ☐

Types of Map: Natural Resources

The Earth is filled with natural resources. These resources include fertile land, forests, water, metals, and minerals. Countries use natural resources to develop their economies. Often, countries that are rich in some resources, such as metals, may trade them with other countries. They can then buy the resources they do not have.

The continent of Africa is very rich in natural resources. This map shows the resources that are found there. Study the map and answer the questions below.

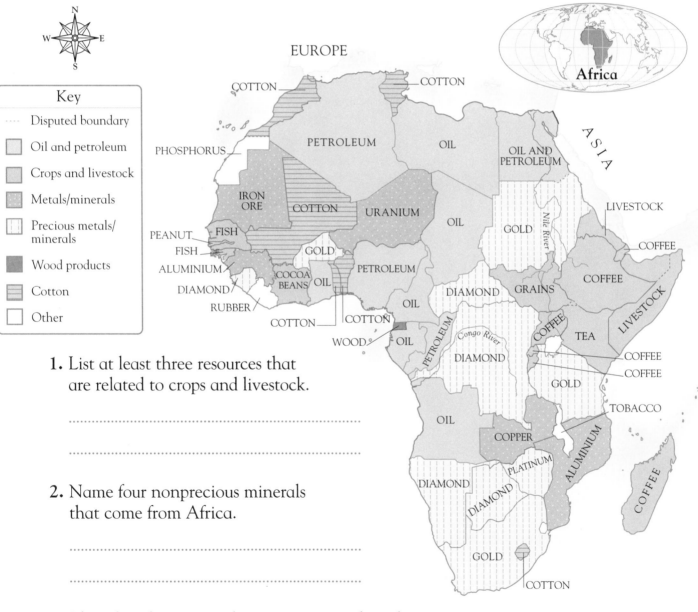

1. List at least three resources that are related to crops and livestock.

....

....

2. Name four nonprecious minerals that come from Africa.

....

....

3. Identify at least one other resource noted on the map.

....

FACTS

Weather maps show the weather of an area for a particular period of time. They can show weather and temperature predictions, such as sunshine or rainfall. Some weather maps forecast the weather of a large area, such as a country or continent. Weather maps are important for travelers and pilots to know the weather of where they are and where they are going.

Study this weather map showing the highest temperature forecast (in °F) for many cities in the United States in the month of August in 2015. Then answer the questions below.

1. Which city had the highest temperature? What was the temperature predicted?

....

2. One city located on the west coast was expected to have a rainy and cool day. Name this city and the temperature predicted for it.

....

3. One northern city's high temperature was expected to be in the 60s. Name the city and the temperature predicted for it.

....

4. List the six US cities that were expected to hit 100°F.

....

....

Key	
★	Country capital
★	State capital
•	Major city
〜	Lake
☀	Sunny
⛅	Rainy
☁	Cloudy
⛅	Partly cloudy

United States: Physical Features

FACTS

The United States of America is the third-largest country in the world. It has varied natural features, such as the fertile Great Plains, the five Great Lakes, and the Rocky Mountains. The country also has many dry and sandy deserts, green valleys, and dense swamps.

Study this physical map of the United States and then circle the correct answer below.

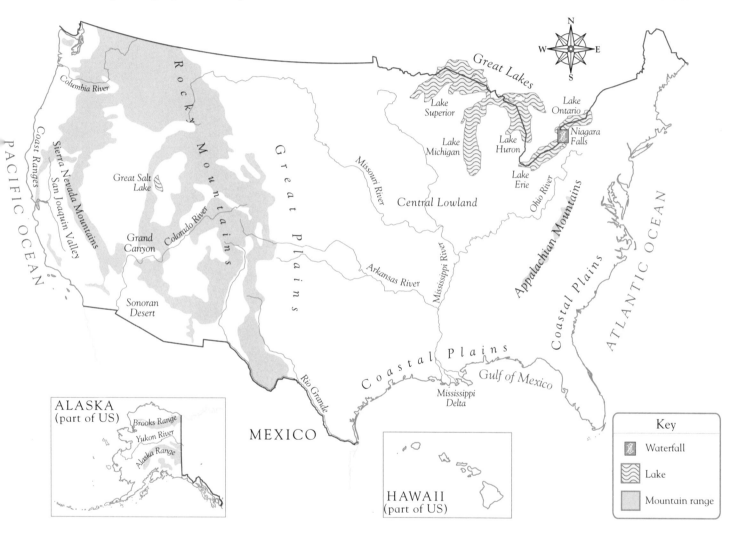

1. Which river flows through the Grand Canyon?
a. Rio Grande
b. Colorado River

2. In which coastal region is the San Joaquin Valley located?
a. East coast
b. West coast

3. Which of these areas would be ideal for farming?
a. Great Plains
b. Great Lakes

United States: Political Divisions

The capital of the United States of America is Washington, D.C. It is where the branches of the US government are located. In addition to the national capital, all 50 US states have their own capital cities, too. These state capitals are cities in which state governments make their laws and regulations.

This map shows the capital cities of the 48 contiguous or connected states in the US. Use this map to write the capital cities for the states listed below.

State Name	Capital City
Texas	
North Dakota	
Wisconsin	
Nevada	
Maine	

Key	
★	Country capital
⋆	State capital
〰	Lake

In 1959, Alaska and Hawaii became the 49th and 50th states of the US. These two are the only US states that are not connected to the US mainland. Alaska is the largest US state and has very cold winters because of its location near the Arctic Circle. In contrast, Hawaii is a series of small islands in the Pacific Ocean. It has a warm climate all year round.

Study these maps of Alaska and Hawaii. Using these maps and information from above, write down three similarities and three differences between these states. **Note:** The first one has been done for you.

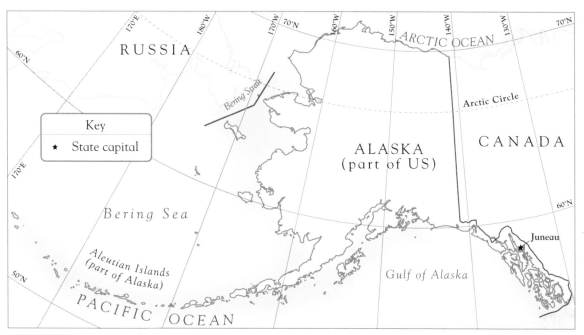

1. Alaska and Hawaii are similar in these ways:

1. Both have borders on the Pacific Ocean.

....

....

....

2. Alaska and Hawaii are different in these ways:

1. Alaska borders Canada but Hawaii does not border any other country.

....

....

FACTS

Maps can show us the difference between the world as it was years ago and the world as it is today. Ancient maps show what people thought the world looked like hundreds of years ago. These ancient maps changed as explorers discovered unknown lands and new information was added to these maps to make them more accurate. The latest maps show all the countries and cities that are known. Comparing these maps can reveal what has changed over time.

The maps on the facing page show the east coast of the United States. The first map shows the 13 British colonies in 1775, just before the American Revolutionary War. The second map shows the east coast of the United States as it is today. Study the maps and then answer the questions below.

1. The state of New Hampshire was larger in 1775 than it is today. Which state was later carved out from New Hampshire to make a new state?

....

2. In the map of 1775, the northernmost colony belonged to Massachusetts. It later became a new state. What is the name of that state?

....

3. The area under West Florida is now part of the states of Alabama and Mississippi. Find two more differences between the map of 1775 map and today's map. Write them below.

....

....

....

....

Key
- Lake
- British colonies
- Other British territories
- Other foreign areas

Map of 1775

4. Name the seven colonies on the map of 1775 that have similar borders to that of the states as they are drawn in today's US map.

....

....

....

....

....

....

Today's map

★ United States: Time Zones

As the Earth rotates, half of it points toward the sun and the other half points away. In some parts of the world, it is daytime, while in other it is nighttime. Time zones were created to know the time in different places around the world. The US crosses six time zones, four of which are in mainland US. So, when it is 9 AM in the Eastern Time Zone, it will be 8 AM in the Central Time Zone, 7 AM in the Mountain Time Zone, and 6 AM in the Pacific Time Zone. As for the other two states, it will be 5 AM in most of Alaska—the part that is in the Alaskan Time Zone. At the same moment, in standard time, it will be 4 AM in Hawaii, which is located in the Hawaii-Aleutian Time Zone.

This map shows the time zones in the US. Imagine that you are in Columbia, South Carolina, and need to call friends in other cities. If it is 3 PM in Columbia, write what time it will be in the cities listed below.

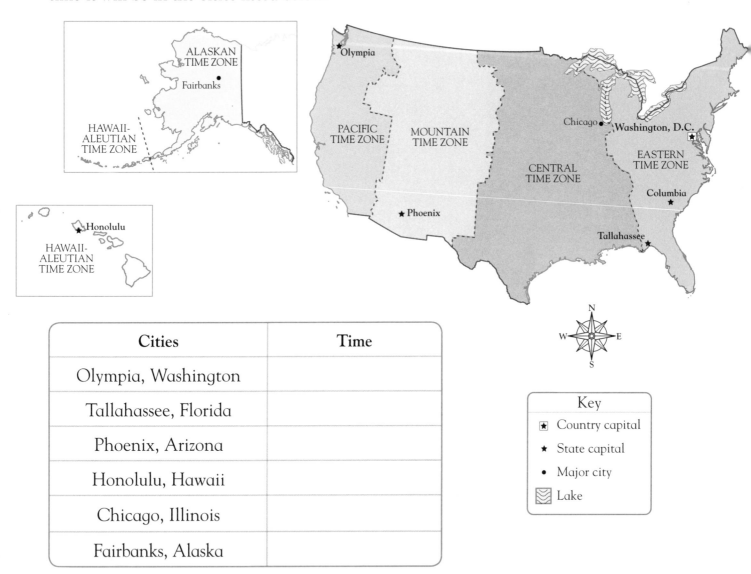

Cities	Time
Olympia, Washington	
Tallahassee, Florida	
Phoenix, Arizona	
Honolulu, Hawaii	
Chicago, Illinois	
Fairbanks, Alaska	

Key
★ Country capital
★ State capital
• Major city
≋ Lake

Geography and Earth's Future

We live on a beautiful planet. It is filled with many natural features and a variety of plants and animals. However, there are many things that pose a danger to the Earth and its future. It is up to us, the people of Earth, to work together and find ways to protect our planet.

We can protect the Earth in many ways. Take a look at the sentences below about saving the Earth's resources. Use words from the word box to complete them.

Bag	Donate
Clean	Pollution
Paper	Electricity

1. Small changes, such as writing on both sides of a piece of ...., can help protect the Earth.

2. Walking, cycling, or using public transportation can lower the amount of .... in the air.

3. Water is crucial to life on Earth, so we should keep rivers and lakes ....

4. When leaving a room, turn off the lights. This will help save ....

5. Instead of throwing out old books and clothing, ... them.

6. At the supermarket, instead of getting a paper or plastic one, bring your own ....

Certificate

4th Grade

Congratulations to

....

for successfully
finishing this book.

GOOD JOB!

You're a star.

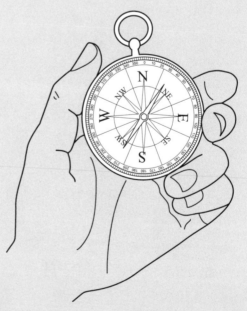

Date

....

Answer Section
with Parents' Notes

This book is intended to support the geography concepts that are taught to your child in the fourth grade. It includes activities that test your child's knowledge of the world around him or her. By working through this book, your child will be able to learn basic geography concepts in a fun and informative way.

Contents

These activities are intended to be completed by a child with adult support. The topics covered are as follows:

- The natural world and the world built by humans;
- Maps and globes;
- Map projections;
- Hemispheres;
- Oceans;
- Latitude and longitude;
- Informational maps—population, rainfall, and natural resources;
- Physical features—mountains, rivers, deserts, and rain forests;
- Continents and countries;
- Important regions of the world.

How to Help Your Child

As you work through the pages with your child, make sure he or she understands what each activity requires. Read the facts and instructions aloud. Encourage questions and reinforce observations that will build confidence and increase active participation in classes at school.

By working with your child, you will understand how he or she thinks and learns. When appropriate, use props and objects from daily life to help your child make connections with the world outside.

If an activity seems too challenging, encourage your child to try another page. You can also give encouragement by praising progress as he or she gives a correct answer and completes an activity. Good luck, and remember to have fun!

4

★ What is Geography?

Geography helps us understand more about the planet on which we live. Geography tells us about the natural world, such as continents, mountains, oceans, and rivers. It also makes us aware of things built by humans, such as cities, bridges, and tunnels.

How well do you know your planet? Look at the numbers on this map of the Earth and the names in the word box below. Write the name for each number.
Note: The first one has been done for you.

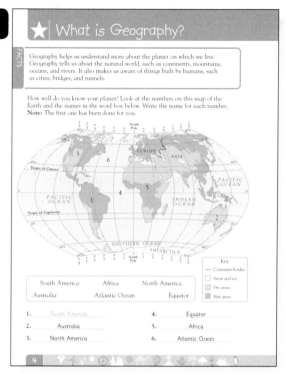

| South America | Africa | North America |
| Australia | Atlantic Ocean | Equator |

1. _South America_   4. _Equator_
2. _Australia_   5. _Africa_
3. _North America_   6. _Atlantic Ocean_

Offer your child examples of the types of questions geography answers. Wonder aloud: How far are we from the North Pole? Where are the world's tallest mountains? Why do some rivers flow into oceans while others flow into lakes? Explain that geography answers these and many other questions.

5

Our Changing World ★

The surface of the Earth is covered with landmasses, oceans, deserts, forests, and other natural features. Most of these have been here for millions of years, but things have changed over time. People have built cities and highways. Some forests have been cut down to make way for buildings. Storms, floods, or fire have also changed the way some places look.

Below are some landmarks from around the United States (US). Write **N** for a natural feature and **B** for something built by humans.

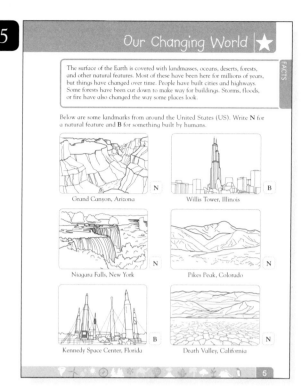

Grand Canyon, Arizona — N
Willis Tower, Illinois — B
Niagara Falls, New York — N
Pikes Peak, Colorado — N
Kennedy Space Center, Florida — B
Death Valley, California — N

As a parent, you know that change is constant. Pick a community change you have noticed (the weather, a new building under construction, a road being paved) and point it out to your child. Ask, "Have you seen anything new?" Then discuss if people or nature changed those things.

6

★ How Maps Work

Maps show where places are located. They explain where a place is in relation to other places. For example, a city map can help you locate a museum by showing that it is around the corner from a place you know, such as a library. City maps include street names and numbers.

Look at this map of Sacramento, California. Use the map to answer the questions below.

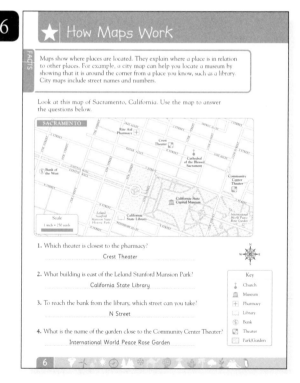

Key
† Church
🏛 Museum
✛ Pharmacy
▢ Library
$ Bank
▢ Theater
▢ Park/Garden

1. Which theater is closest to the pharmacy?
   Crest Theater

2. What building is east of the Leland Stanford Mansion Park?
   California State Library

3. To reach the bank from the library, which street can you take?
   N Street

4. What is the name of the garden close to the Community Center Theater?
   International World Peace Rose Garden

Encourage your child to make a map. It could be a map of your town, your home, or even your child's room. Decide what information you need to get started on the map, such as what to show, where things are in relation to each other, and so on.

Compass Directions ★

To use most maps, we need to know the four major directions—north, south, east, and west. Wherever we are on Earth, only one direction leads to the North Pole—north! South is exactly the opposite direction. The sun appears every morning in the east and disappears in the west. Knowing a map's compass directions shows which way you should go to reach a certain place.

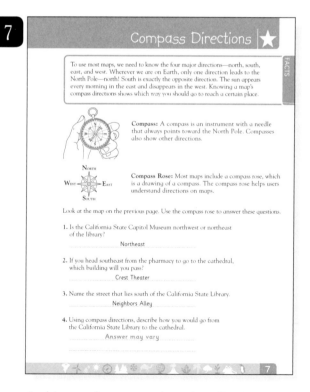

Compass: A compass is an instrument with a needle that always points toward the North Pole. Compasses also show other directions.

Compass Rose: Most maps include a compass rose, which is a drawing of a compass. The compass rose helps users understand directions on maps.

Look at the map on the previous page. Use the compass rose to answer these questions.

1. Is the California State Capitol Museum northwest or northeast of the library?
   Northeast

2. If you head southeast from the pharmacy to go to the cathedral, which building will you pass?
   Crest Theater

3. Name the street that lies south of the California State Library.
   Neighbors Alley

4. Using compass directions, describe how you would go from the California State Library to the cathedral.
   Answer may vary

As this page shows, maps depend on direction. Ask your child to explain the four main directions to you. Then, working together, determine the locations of north, south, east, and west from your home. Check your findings against a map of your community.

★ Map Key

FACTS

Maps show information using symbols. These symbols are markers that represent streets, parks, bodies of water, highways, and so on. In the map of a state, a star may stand for the capital city and solid dots may stand for the major cities. These symbols and their explanations are included in boxes called keys or legends.

Study this map of the US state of Florida, with its many symbols. Each number is pointing to a symbol. Use the key and write the correct word for each symbol.

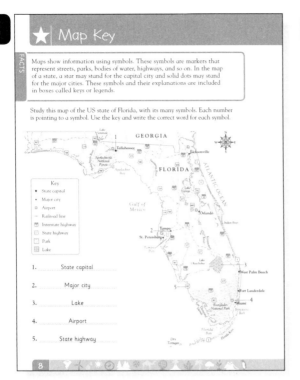

1. _____ State capital

2. _____ Major city

3. _____ Lake

4. _____ Airport

5. _____ State highway

Maps use symbols to identify places. Review some maps and their symbols. Ask your child to list places he or she would like noted on community maps—computer store, toy store, library, pizza place? Then draw symbols that could be added to your local map.

9

Map Scale ★

FACTS

Every map is smaller than the place it shows. To make it possible to show big places on a map, mapmakers use a tool called scale. The scale is a line that tells us how much a certain distance on the map represents.

This map of the state of Tennessee shows its many cities. Use the scale above the map and a ruler to find answers to the questions. Then, circle the correct answers below.

Scale
1 inch = 75 miles

(map of Tennessee)

1. How far is Dyersburg from Maryville?
   a. 260 miles   **b. 300 miles**

2. Calculate the approximate distance between Nashville and Memphis.
   a. 188 miles   b. 200 miles

3. What is the approximate distance between Chattanooga and Cookeville?
   a. 75 miles   b. 85 miles

4. Which distance is longer?
   a. Memphis to Lawrenceburg   **b. Franklin to Knoxville**

Maps can cover either tiny or vast areas. Demonstrate that difference by comparing a world map, a national map, and a town map. Explain that the three are similar in size but that their scales are very different. Then have your child read aloud the scale information for each map.

10

★ Grids and City Maps

FACTS

Cities can be complicated places with hundreds of streets. To help people find streets and buildings, maps include a grid and an index. A grid is a series of crisscrossing lines that divide the map into boxes. One side of the map is labeled with letters and the other side with numbers. You can find locations using the grid numbers, which are listed in the map's index.

The map below shows a part of the city of Philadelphia, Pennsylvania, and some of its landmarks. Use it to answer the questions below.

(grid map of Philadelphia)

Key
- Interstate highway
- Building
- Museum
- Bell
- Mint
- Park/Garden

1. This building is between Race Street and Cherry Street, just west of 5th Street. What is its grid number and the name of the place?
   C1; National Constitution Center

2. Just south of Chestnut Street, between 5th and 6th streets, is a building where an important document was signed. What is its grid number and what is the name of the building?
   C3; Independence Hall

3. In grid D3, between Market Street and Chestnut Street, there is a building named after a famous person. Name it.
   Benjamin Franklin Museum

This page discusses how grids (series of crisscrossing lines) help people find locations on maps. In fact, most maps of cities, towns, even amusement parks, use a letter-and-number grid system. Search for examples of these grids and share them with your child.

11

Maps of Countries ★

FACTS

More than 190 countries exist in the world today, and there is a map for each one. Country maps show us the shape of the country's borders, the names of its big cities, and the location of important natural features and landmarks built by humans.

This map shows Slovenia, a small country in southern Europe, surrounded by Italy, Austria, Hungary, and Croatia. Two million people live in Slovenia's cities and countryside. Use the map to circle the correct answers below.

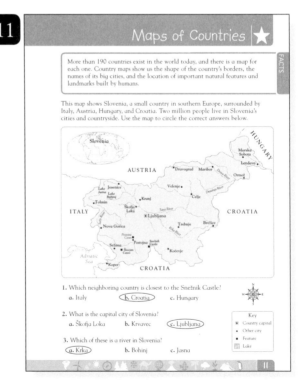

Key
- Country capital
- Other city
- Feature
- Lake

1. Which neighboring country is closest to the Snežnik Castle?
   a. Italy   **b. Croatia**   c. Hungary

2. What is the capital city of Slovenia?
   a. Škofja Loka   b. Krvavec   **c. Ljubljana**

3. Which of these is a river in Slovenia?
   a. Krka   b. Bohinj   c. Jasna

Show your child a map of the United States. Discuss the decisions that had to be made about the map: Are all cities included? Is every river shown? Are highways included or not? Find another map of the US. Invite your child to find differences between the two.

★ Maps and Globes

FACTS

Earth can be shown using flat maps and globes. Globes are shaped like the Earth, and they show the planet more accurately than flat maps. Although both are useful, maps are easier to carry. While flat maps are great for finding directions, globes are best for understanding how all the parts of our world make up one planet.

Look at the globe and the flat map below. Then read the statements below and check (✓) if each one is **true** or **false**.

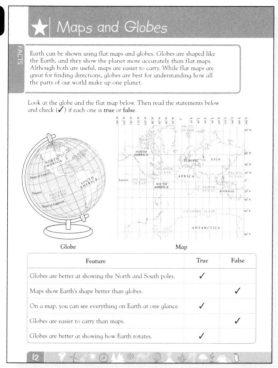

Globe   Map

Feature	True	False
Globes are better at showing the North and South poles.	✓	
Maps show Earth's shape better than globes.		✓
On a map, you can see everything on Earth at one glance.	✓	
Globes are easier to carry than maps.		✓
Globes are better at showing how Earth rotates.	✓	

Look at a globe and a world map and discuss which is more useful (and why). If you do not have a globe, get a ball. Then review the drawing of the globe on this page and ask your child to describe how a flat drawing differs from a round object.

Map Projections ★

FACTS

Maps and globes show the same Earth. It is, however, impossible to represent perfectly a round world on a flat map. Every world map shows something inaccurately. It could be the land's size or shape, or the distances between places. Mapmakers use different techniques, called projections, to show the curved surface of the Earth. Here are two of them:
Mercator Projection: This projection shows directions well. However, the places far from the equator are distorted and look too large.
Interrupted Projection: This projection presents the shapes and sizes of land accurately, but the distance and directions shown are not true or accurate.

Look at the Mercator and Interrupted map projections. Then read the statements and check (✓) if each one is **true** or **false**.

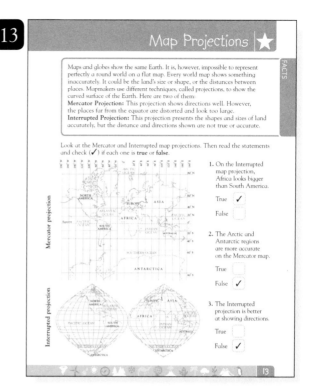

Mercator projection

Interrupted projection

1. On the Interrupted map projection, Africa looks bigger than South America.

   True ✓

   False ☐

2. The Arctic and Antarctic regions are more accurate on the Mercator map.

   True ☐

   False ✓

3. The Interrupted projection is better at showing directions.

   True ☐

   False ✓

Showing the round Earth on a flat surface is challenging. With your child, pick something round (a baseball, apple, or globe, for instance) and draw it. Then discuss the problems of mapmaking and drawing. To see interesting solutions by mapmakers, search online for images of "map projections."

★ Latitude

FACTS

Latitudes are imaginary lines that run horizontally across the Earth. They mark where something is in the north and south of our planet. They measure distance in degrees (°). The equator is latitude zero as it lies midway between the North and South poles. The North Pole is 90° north. The South Pole is 90° south. The latitudes in between are 1° to 89° north or south.

Iowa is a state located in the central United States. This map shows latitude lines of 41°, 42°, and 43° going east and west across Iowa. Use the map to answer the questions below.

Key
• State capital
• Major city

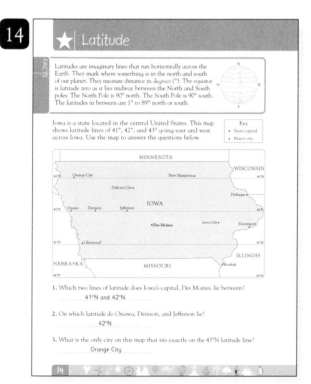

1. Which two lines of latitude does Iowa's capital, Des Moines, lie between?
   41°N and 42°N

2. On which latitude do Onawa, Denison, and Jefferson lie?
   42°N

3. What is the only city on this map that sits exactly on the 43°N latitude line?
   Orange City

After your child has read this page, see if he or she can explain that latitude is a series of lines that help us locate places on Earth. Then review a world map and point out the latitudes of various locations.

Longitude ★

FACTS

Longitudes are imaginary lines that run from north to south across maps of the Earth. They come together at the North and South poles. The prime meridian is the 0° longitude, which passes through Greenwich, England. The Earth is divided into 360° of longitude—180° east of the prime meridian and 180° west.

This map shows the state of Nebraska, which is just west of Iowa. Nebraska has longitudes ranging between 95° and 104° west. Use the map to answer the questions below.

Key
• State capital
• Major city

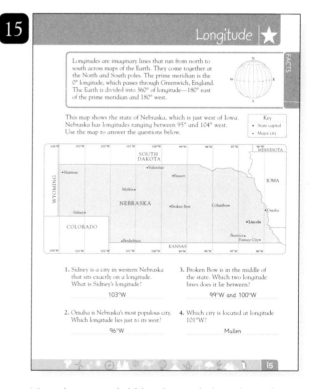

1. Sidney is a city in western Nebraska that sits exactly on a longitude. What is Sidney's longitude?
   103°W

2. Omaha is Nebraska's most populous city. Which longitude lies just to its west?
   96°W

3. Broken Bow is in the middle of the state. Which two longitude lines does it lie between?
   99°W and 100°W

4. Which city is located at longitude 101°W?
   Mullen

Now that your child has learned about latitude and longitude, try finding your home's coordinates. Use a large map for a rough estimate. Next, search the Internet for a more precise answer. This website is a good resource: http://www.latlong.net/.

★ Special Latitude Lines

FACTS

The equator is the 0° latitude. It is an imaginary line that lies midway between the North Pole and the South Pole. It divides the Earth into the northern and southern hemispheres. Two other special latitude lines are the Tropic of Cancer, at 23.5° north, and the Tropic of Capricorn, at 23.5° south. Between these two lines are the regions called the tropics, which are the hottest areas on Earth.

This map of the world shows the special latitude lines. Use it to answer the questions below.

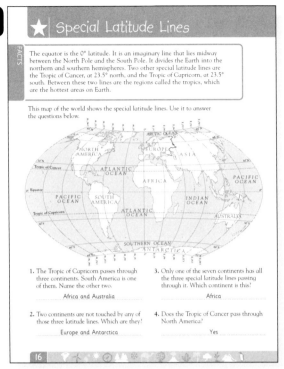

1. The Tropic of Capricorn passes through three continents. South America is one of them. Name the other two.

   Africa and Australia

2. Two continents are not touched by any of those three latitude lines. Which are they?

   Europe and Antarctica

3. Only one of the seven continents has all the three special latitude lines passing through it. Which continent is this?

   Africa

4. Does the Tropic of Cancer pass through North America?

   Yes

Ask your child to trace the Tropic of Cancer across a world map and name some countries it crosses. Then do the same with the equator and the Tropic of Capricorn. Do you know anyone who lives close to any of these (imaginary) latitude lines?

Hemispheres ★

FACTS

Hemisphere means "half of a sphere." Imaginary lines divide the Earth into four hemispheres. The equator, which is the 0° latitude, divides the Earth into the northern and southern hemispheres. The prime meridian, which is the 0° longitude, divides the Earth into the eastern and western hemispheres.

Look at these maps showing the four hemispheres. Read the statements below and check (✓) if each one is **true** or **false**.

Northern hemisphere (N)   **Western hemisphere (W)**

Southern hemisphere (S)   **Eastern hemisphere (E)**

1. Most of Earth's land can be found in the southern hemisphere.

   True ☐   False ✓

2. Most of Europe is located in the western hemisphere.

   True ☐   False ✓

3. Antarctica is located in all the four hemispheres.

   True ☐   False ✓

4. No continent is located only in one hemisphere.

   True ✓   False ☐

To further reinforce the concept of various hemispheres, use an orange or other roundish fruit. Show your child that you could slice it round vertically or horizontally—in each case creating different hemispheres, just as this page discusses.

★ Oceans

FACTS

From space, Earth looks like a blue ball. This is because about 70 percent of its surface is water. The five salty oceans—the Pacific, Atlantic, Indian, Southern, and Arctic oceans—make up 96 percent of all water on Earth. Other bodies of water, such as freshwater lakes, ponds, and rivers, make up just four percent.

The oceans on Earth are actually one giant body of water that interrupts the continents. Study this map showing the oceans and answer the questions below.

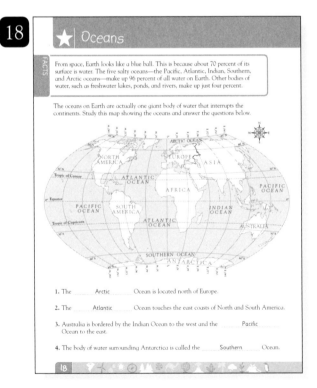

1. The ____Arctic____ Ocean is located north of Europe.

2. The ____Atlantic____ Ocean touches the east coasts of North and South America.

3. Australia is bordered by the Indian Ocean to the west and the ____Pacific____ Ocean to the east.

4. The body of water surrounding Antarctica is called the ____Southern____ Ocean.

What makes oceans different from other bodies of water? If your family has visited an ocean, talk about the experience and discuss the difference between lakes and rivers. If you haven't, compile a list of ocean attributes (size; depth; never-ending waves; salty water, etc.) and compare it to local waters.

Continents ★

FACTS

Continents are the biggest masses of land on Earth. There are seven continents, with Asia being the largest. The other six, in order of size, are Africa, North America, South America, Antarctica, Europe, and Australia. Six of these are home to millions of people. The seventh, Antarctica, is a frozen continent and has a very small population of scientists living there to do research.

Study this map showing Earth's seven continents. Then answer the questions below.

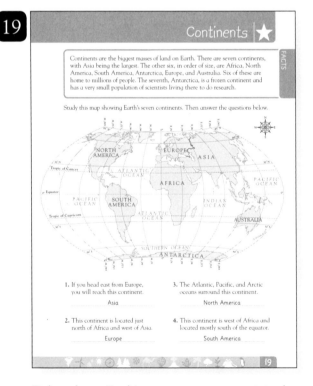

1. If you head east from Europe, you will reach this continent.

   Asia

2. This continent is located just north of Africa and west of Asia.

   Europe

3. The Atlantic, Pacific, and Arctic oceans surround this continent.

   North America

4. This continent is west of Africa and located mostly south of the equator.

   South America

Did you know Earth's continents were once joined in a supercontinent and then drifted apart? The jigsaw-puzzle-style evidence can still be seen on maps: Look how South America's east coast and Africa's west coast seem to fit together. To learn more, search online for "Pangaea."

★ North America

FACTS

North America is Earth's third-largest continent. Climate varies widely across North America. Areas near the Arctic Circle have a very cold climate, the middle regions are mostly temperate, and the southern areas are tropical. Around 600 million people live on this continent. There are more than 300 million people in the United States, 122 million in Mexico, and 35 million in Canada.

Study this map of North America showing its countries and some physical features. Then read the descriptions. On the map, write the letter next to the place that matches each description.

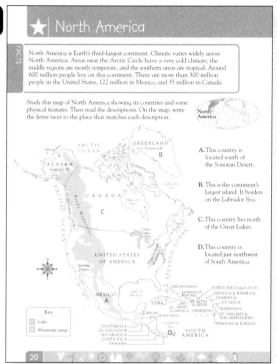

A. This country is located south of the Sonoran Desert.

B. This is the continent's largest island. It borders on the Labrador Sea.

C. This country lies north of the Great Lakes.

D. This country is located just northwest of South America.

At first glance, North America seems to include only three large countries. In fact, it is a diverse continent encompassing Greenland, Central America, and the island nations of the Caribbean. Invite your child to pick one of those lesser-known places and find out about its people and geography.

South America ★

FACTS

South America is Earth's fourth-largest continent. It is a land of contrasts. It is home to the snow-peaked Andes Mountains and the largest rain forest on Earth, the Amazon. South America begins just north of the equator but extends the farthest south of any continent. About 400 million people live in its 12 countries, including large ones, such as Brazil and Argentina, and smaller ones, such as Suriname and Ecuador.

Study this map of South America showing its 12 countries. Then using this map, write the name of the country that matches each description.

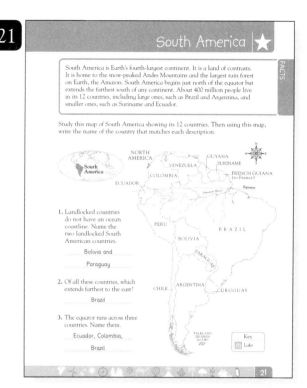

1. Landlocked countries do not have an ocean coastline. Name the two landlocked South American countries.

   Bolivia and

   Paraguay

2. Of all these countries, which extends furthest to the east?

   Brazil

3. The equator runs across three countries. Name them.

   Ecuador, Colombia,

   Brazil

Spanish is the main language of eight South American countries, but not of the other four. For another example of South America's diversity, help your child to discover the official languages of Brazil, French Guiana, Guyana, and Suriname.

★ Africa

FACTS

Africa is Earth's second-largest continent. It has more than 1 billion people spread across more than 50 countries. Africa is famous for its natural features, such as the Sahara—Earth's largest desert—and the Nile—Earth's longest river. Africa also has unusual wildlife, such as giraffes, elephants, and zebras.

Study this map showing some natural features of Africa. Read the statements below and check (✓) if each one is true or false.

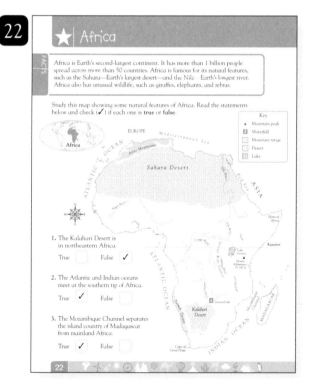

1. The Kalahari Desert is in northeastern Africa.

   True ☐   False ✓

2. The Atlantic and Indian oceans meet at the southern tip of Africa.

   True ✓   False ☐

3. The Mozambique Channel separates the island country of Madagascar from mainland Africa.

   True ✓   False ☐

This map shows significant physical features of Africa, but does not label its fifty-plus countries. Using a political map, ask your child to find and write the names of a few large African countries, such as Algeria, Angola, Ethiopia, Libya, Niger, Nigeria, Sudan, and South Africa.

Asia ★

FACTS

Asia is Earth's largest continent. It stretches all the way from the cold grasslands of Siberia to the rain forests of Vietnam. Four billion people live in Asia. This is more than the number of people living on all the other continents combined. Asia also has Earth's tallest mountain chain, the Himalayas.

Unscramble the names of Asia's four most populated countries. Use this map of Asia to help you.

Scrambled Words	Country Name
Incha	China
Niadi	India
Napikast	Pakistan
Gladabensh	Bangladesh

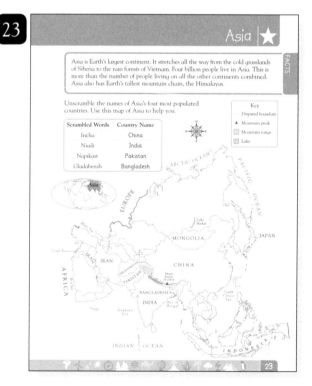

This page uses a word game to introduce children to four of the world's most populous countries. After helping your child unscramble the words, discover more about one of these growing Asian countries.

★ Australia

FACTS

Australia is Earth's smallest continent. Although Australia is about the same size as the mainland United States, its population is less than that of California. The continent is famous for its wildlife, which includes kangaroos, koalas, and wallabies.

This map shows Australia and some nearby countries. Study the map and then circle the correct answers.

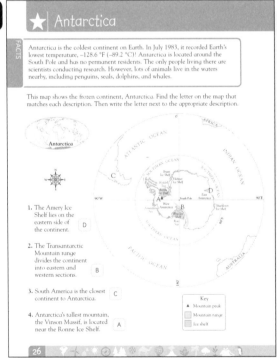

1. Which of these oceans surround Australia?
   a. Indian and Pacific oceans
   b. Atlantic and Indian oceans
   c. Arctic and Southern oceans

2. Which continent is closest to Australia?
   a. North America
   b. Asia
   c. South America

3. If you traveled southeast from Australia, which country would you reach?
   a. Indonesia
   b. Japan
   c. New Zealand

Many children know Australia, its remarkable wildlife, including kangaroos, koalas, and duck-billed platypuses. Help your child learn about other intriguing Australian animals, such as dingoes, quokkas, wombats, and Tasmanian devils.

Europe ★

FACTS

Europe is the second-smallest continent. It is connected to Earth's biggest continent, Asia. The Ural Mountains act as a natural border between the two. With 750 million residents, Europe is Earth's third-most populated continent.

This map shows four European capital cities. Imagine that you are traveling to each of them. Read the descriptions, and number the capital cities on the map in the order visited. **Note:** The first one has been done for you.

1. Your trip begins in Athens, the capital of Greece. Find the number 1.

2. You fly west across the Mediterranean Sea to Madrid, the capital of the southwestern country of Spain.

3. Next, you take a train to Berlin, the capital of the central European nation of Germany.

4. Finally, you drive east into the large neighboring country of Poland to its capital city, Warsaw.

Key
Disputed boundary
● Country capital

The activity on this page takes children on a tour of some European capital cities. Make this activity more interesting by finding and sharing with your child photos or videos of Athens, Warsaw, Madrid, and Berlin.

★ Antarctica

FACTS

Antarctica is the coldest continent on Earth. In July 1983, it recorded Earth's lowest temperature, −128.6 °F (−89.2 °C)! Antarctica is located around the South Pole and has no permanent residents. The only people living there are scientists conducting research. However, lots of animals live in the waters nearby, including penguins, seals, dolphins, and whales.

This map shows the frozen continent, Antarctica. Find the letter on the map that matches each description. Then write the letter next to the appropriate description.

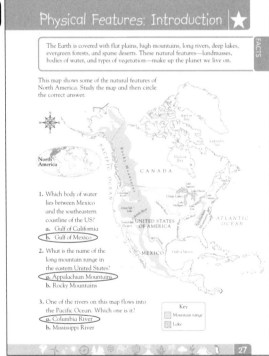

1. The Amery Ice Shelf lies on the eastern side of the continent. **D**

2. The Transantarctic Mountain range divides the continent into eastern and western sections. **B**

3. South America is the closest continent to Antarctica. **C**

4. Antarctica's tallest mountain, the Vinson Massif, is located near the Ronne Ice Shelf. **A**

Key
▲ Mountain peak
Mountain range
Ice shelf

Talk to your child about the icy continent of Antarctica by comparing the South Pole to the North Pole. Ask, "Which pole is surrounded by land?"; "Which by water?"; "Near which pole would you find polar bears?"; and "Where will you find penguins?"

Physical Features: Introduction ★

FACTS

The Earth is covered with flat plains, high mountains, long rivers, deep lakes, evergreen forests, and sparse deserts. These natural features—landmasses, bodies of water, and types of vegetation—make up the planet we live on.

This map shows some of the natural features of North America. Study the map and then circle the correct answer.

1. Which body of water lies between Mexico and the southeastern coastline of the US?
   a. Gulf of California
   b. Gulf of Mexico

2. What is the name of the long mountain range in the eastern United States?
   a. Appalachian Mountains
   b. Rocky Mountains

3. One of the rivers on this map flows into the Pacific Ocean. Which one is it?
   a. Columbia River
   b. Mississippi River

Key
Mountain range
Lake

Earth's natural features often pose challenges to human activity. Take a walk with your child and look for examples of natural features, such as hills, forests, and rivers. Then discuss some ways in which people adapt to their surroundings (building bridges, restricting activities, and protecting wildlife).

★ Physical Features: Lakes

FACTS

Lakes are bodies of water that are surrounded by land on all sides. Most lakes are freshwater, though there are a few saltwater lakes. Many lakes were formed by the movement of giant sheets of ice, known as glaciers, many thousands of years ago. Unlike water in oceans and rivers, the water in lakes does not move much.

The state of Minnesota contains more than 12,000 lakes bigger than 10 acres. Look at this map of Minnesota showing some of its lakes. Then write their names to match the descriptions.

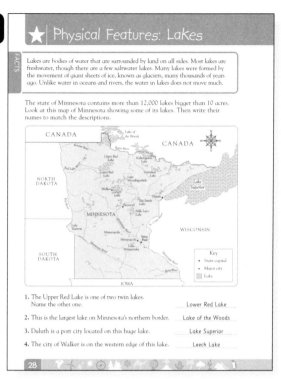

1. The Upper Red Lake is one of two twin lakes.
   Name the other one. — Lower Red Lake

2. This is the largest lake on Minnesota's northern border. — Lake of the Woods

3. Duluth is a port city located on this huge lake. — Lake Superior

4. The city of Walker is on the western edge of this lake. — Leech Lake

Lakes come in all sizes, shapes, and are found in most places. The Great Lakes, which extend from Minnesota to New York, form the world's largest freshwater system. On a US map, help your child locate the five lakes and guess which is the biggest (Superior) and which is the smallest (Ontario).

Physical Features: Rivers ★

FACTS

Rivers are large flowing bodies of freshwater. They usually start in mountains or hills. Some are fed by rainwater or melting snow. From earliest times, rivers have provided people with drinking water and places to wash, catch fish, and travel by boat. All rivers flow into other, larger bodies of water, such as oceans, seas, lakes, and other rivers.

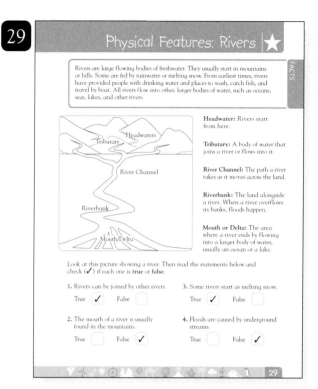

Headwater: Rivers start from here.

Tributary: A body of water that joins a river or flows into it.

River Channel: The path a river takes as it moves across the land.

Riverbank: The land alongside a river. When a river overflows its banks, floods happen.

Mouth or Delta: The area where a river ends by flowing into a larger body of water, usually an ocean or a lake.

Look at this picture showing a river. Then read the statements below and check (✔) if each one is true or false.

1. Rivers can be joined by other rivers.
   True ✔   False ☐

2. The mouth of a river is usually found in the mountains.
   True ☐   False ✔

3. Some rivers start as melting snow.
   True ✔   False ☐

4. Floods are caused by underground streams.
   True ☐   False ✔

Choose a river in your area and find a map that includes it. After reviewing the river vocabulary on this page, such as headwaters, tributary, riverbank, and delta, work with your child to identify as many of these as possible for your local river.

★ Physical Features: Mountains

FACTS

Areas that are the high points on Earth's surface are called mountains. While some mountains slope up gradually, many others rise steeply. The Himalayas in Asia are the tallest mountain range on Earth. Mount Everest is the highest peak. It is more than 29,000 feet above sea level.

The highest mountain peaks on the seven continents are called "The Seven Summits." Look at the list below showing the heights of these peaks and the continents where they are found. Then find the mountains in the word search below.

Continent	Mountain	Height (in feet)
Asia	Everest	29,029
South America	Aconcagua	22,831
North America	Denali	20,310
Africa	Kilimanjaro	19,341
Europe	Elbrus	18,510
Antarctica	Vinson Massif	16,050
Australia	Kosciuszko	7,310

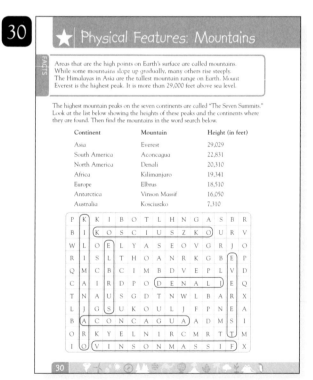

This activity talks about the highest peak in every continent. In 2015, one of these peaks, Mount McKinley, underwent a name change to "Denali," meaning "great one." Other peaks, including the Everest, also have native names. Help your child to research how a specific peak got its name.

Physical Features: Deserts ★

FACTS

Deserts are areas that receive less than 10 inches of rain in a year. Deserts can be hot and sandy or cold and frozen. Antarctica is a desert. These places are among the most difficult places to live because of the shortage of water and the harsh climate. However, some plants and animals do survive there.

The map and chart locate and describe the Sahara and Gobi deserts. Study them and then compare and contrast them, writing three similarities and three differences.
Note: The first one has been done for you.

Features	Gobi	Sahara
Type of desert	Cold	Hot
Location	Central Asia	North Africa
Size	At 500,000 square miles, it is Earth's fifth-largest desert.	At around 3.3 million square miles, it is Earth's largest desert.
Climate	Very cold winters; temperatures go as low as –40° F (–40 °C). Very hot summers; temperatures can rise above 100° F (37.7 °C).	Cool winters; temperature can go below 32° F (0 °C). In summers, this is one of the hottest places, where temperatures can rise over 134° F (56.6 °C).
Human population	Fewer than 3 people per square mile	Fewer than 1 person per square mile
Animal life	Bactrian (two-hump) camels, antelopes, gazelles, cattle, sheep, and goats	Dromedary (single-hump) camels, gerbils, and desert hedgehogs
Plant life	Some small bushes and desert-grass steppes	Grasses, shrubs, and palm trees only at oases

Similarities	Differences
1. Both deserts have very hot summers	1. Both are home to different types of camel
Answer may vary	Answer may vary

Ask your child, "Why are deserts among the least-populated places on Earth?" Work together to discover what makes deserts such hard places to live. Answers will include lack of water and extreme changes in temperature.

★ Physical Features: Rain Forests

FACTS

Rain forests are dense, damp, tree-filled regions. Although they cover only two percent of the Earth's surface, about half of the Earth's animal and plant species live in rain forests. Rain forest trees help humans by producing a huge amount of the oxygen we breathe in and absorbing carbon dioxide we breathe out. Earth's rain forests are endangered, so it is important that we find ways to protect them.

This map shows where some of the world's most important rain forests are located. Read each description, look at the map and then write the answers.

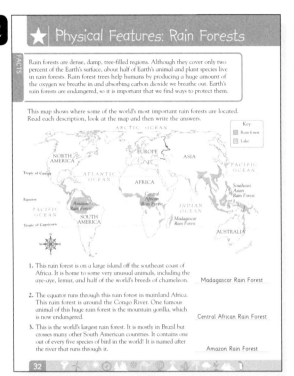

Key
▪ Rain forest
▩ Lake

1. This rain forest is on a large island off the southeast coast of Africa. It is home to some very unusual animals, including the aye-aye, lemur, and half of the world's breeds of chameleon.

Madagascar Rain Forest

2. The equator runs through this rain forest in mainland Africa. This rain forest is around the Congo River. One famous animal of this huge rain forest is the mountain gorilla, which is now endangered.

Central African Rain Forest

3. This is the world's largest rain forest. It is mostly in Brazil but crosses many other South American countries. It contains one out of every five species of bird in the world! It is named after the river that runs through it.

Amazon Rain Forest

This page helps locate tropical rain forests and refers to their importance. Help your child find out more about the role that forests play in human life, and why they are endangered. Then discuss what might be done to protect these vital resources.

Physical Features: Landforms ★

FACTS

Land on Earth takes many forms. There are mountains and valleys, plateaus and canyons. The shape land takes affects the area's climate and its plant and animal life. These landforms were created over millions of years by natural forces.

Canyon, peninsula, plateau, and **valley** are types of landform. Look at the pictures and their descriptions. Then write the correct name of each landform on the dotted line.

This is a very deep, narrow area that is usually found between steep cliffs. It was carved out by a river.

Canyon

This is a body of land surrounded by water on three sides. It is attached at some point to another landform.

Peninsula

This is a landform that rises above its surroundings. It has a broad, flat area at its highest point.

Plateau

This is a long, broad area of land lower than its surroundings. It may have been formed by a glacier or river.

Valley

Some landforms share common characteristics and differ in important ways. Find illustrations for the following pairs: San Fernando Valley and Grand Canyon; Florida and Madagascar; and Mount Everest and Devils Tower. Then help your child understand the similarities and differences.

★ Types of Map: Introduction

FACTS

Maps help us get from one place to another, but that is just one of their uses. Maps show various kinds of information. Informational maps use pictures, symbols, and colors to show facts. For example, a map can show the changes in a region over 100 years.

This map shows the areas where the ruby-throated and rufous hummingbirds can be found on Earth. Study the map and then circle the correct answers.

Key
▩ Lake
▪ Hummingbird zone

1. Which part of North America does not have the ruby-throated and rufous hummingbirds?
   a. Mexico
   b. Greenland

2. Out of the following, which region has hummingbirds in all parts of it?
   a. the western region of the United States
   b. the eastern region of the United States

3. These hummingbirds are found in all of which area?
   a. Central America
   b. The United States

This page shows areas where the wild hummingbirds are found, introducing the idea that many kinds of information can be pictured on maps. Talk to your child about his or her interests and ask, "Could information about that be turned into a map?" and "What would it look like?"

Types of Map: Political Maps ★

FACTS

A political map shows countries, states, cities, or territories. These maps show the government boundaries of these areas and display clearly where these regions begin and end. The boundary decisions are made by governments of countries. Since the word "politics" means "related to government," these maps are called political maps.

Look at this political map of Central America, the tropical region of North America, south of Mexico. Use the map to answer the questions below.

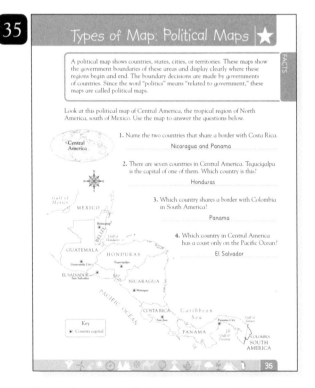

1. Name the two countries that share a border with Costa Rica.

   Nicaragua and Panama

2. There are seven countries in Central America. Tegucigalpa is the capital of one of them. Which country is this?

   Honduras

3. Which country shares a border with Colombia in South America?

   Panama

4. Which country in Central America has a coast only on the Pacific Ocean?

   El Salvador

Key
★ Country capital

Political maps are all about boundaries. Discuss this concept with your child. Ask: "What are boundaries?"; "Why are they important?" You can talk about school districts, bus routes, and property lines as well as state and country borders. Then discuss how these boundaries affect our lives.

36 ★ Types of Map: Physical Maps

Physical maps show the natural features of the Earth. These features include mountains, valleys, plains, rivers, lakes, and other areas of the natural world. Physical maps can show how mountainous or flat an area is. Information from them can be helpful for anyone who wants to farm, live, or build in that area.

Study this physical map of Europe. Then answer the questions.

1. Located north of the Carpathian Mountains, the country of ____Poland____ does not have a major mountain range.

2. ____Andorra____ is a very small country located in the Pyrenees Mountains between Spain and France.

3. The long, narrow country of ____Italy____ has a long coast on the Mediterranean Sea and a mountain range.

Key
Disputed boundary
☒ Lake
☐ Mountain range

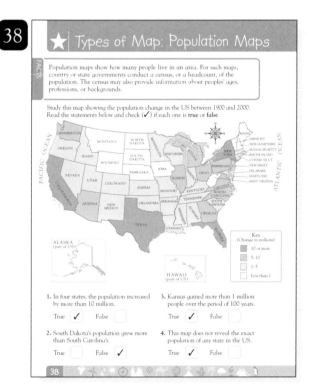

36

Physical maps show how flat or mountainous an area is. Ask your child why this information might be important for farmers, construction workers, pedestrians, and bicyclists. Together, discuss your community's terrain and look for some pictures online.

37 Types of Map: Road Maps ★

Road maps show the locations of cities and the roads that connect there. These maps show the names or numbers of highways in an area. Today, some people have electronic maps that use Global Positioning Systems or GPS, which give information about traffic on the roads, roads under construction, and even show alternate routes to the destination.

Imagine that you are driving from Middletown, a small city in northern Delaware, to visit friends who reside in towns in southern Delaware. Read the descriptions below and decide which roads you will need to take to these cities.

Key
• State capital
• City
▣ Interstate highway
▣ State highway
◯ Highway

1. You start at Middletown and your first stop is the town of Smyrna. You will head south on Highway 896 and join a state highway that will take you right up to Smyrna. Name the state highway that you will take.
____State Highway 13____

2. After a day's stop at Smyrna, you travel to Frederica. After you pass Dover, you have to switch to another road. Which highway is it?
____Highway 1____

3. Dagsboro is your last stop and you will go via Milford. What state highway will take you to your final destination?
____State Highway 113____

37

Children increasingly see grown-ups relying on Global Positioning System (GPS) devices instead of road maps and handwritten directions. If you use GPS, discuss how digital tools have changed travel. Together, come up with disadvantages, as well as advantages, of relying on computers.

38 ★ Types of Map: Population Maps

Population maps show how many people live in an area. For such maps, country or state governments conduct a census, or a headcount, of the population. The census may also provide information about peoples' ages, professions, or backgrounds.

Study this map showing the population change in the US between 1900 and 2000. Read the statements below and check (✔) if each one is **true** or **false**.

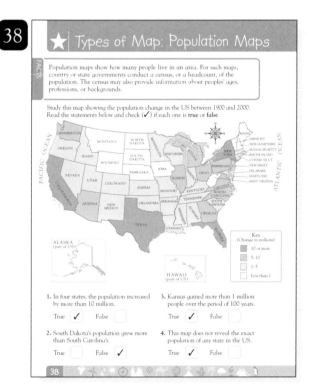

Key
(Change in millions)
■ 10 or more
■ 5–10
■ 1–5
□ Less than 1

1. In four states, the population increased by more than 10 million.
True ✔ False ☐

2. South Dakota's population grew more than South Carolina's.
True ☐ False ✔

3. Kansas gained more than 1 million people over the period of 100 years.
True ✔ False ☐

4. This map does not reveal the exact population of any state in the US.
True ✔ False ☐

38

Can a static map show changes across time? This map demonstrates that the answer is yes. Together with your child, find your state and discuss the information revealed about it on this map. Help your child to research details of the population changes in your state.

39 Types of Map: Natural Resources ★

The Earth is filled with natural resources. These resources include fertile land, forests, water, metals, and minerals. Countries use natural resources to develop their economies. Often, countries that are rich in some resources, such as metals, may trade them with other countries. They can then buy the resources they do not have.

The continent of Africa is very rich in natural resources. This map shows the resources that are found there. Study the map and answer the questions below.

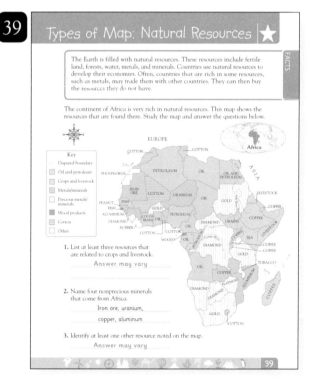

Key
Disputed boundary
☐ Oil and petroleum
☐ Crops and livestock
☐ Metals/minerals
☐ Precious metals/minerals
■ Wood products
☐ Cotton
☐ Other

1. List at least three resources that are related to crops and livestock.
____Answer may vary____

2. Name four nonprecious minerals that come from Africa.
____Iron ore, uranium, copper, aluminum____

3. Identify at least one other resource noted on the map.
____Answer may vary____

39

Natural resource maps show where valuable elements are located. Assess your child's understanding of what a natural resource is, and make a list of other examples such as copper, rubber, grain, and water power. Then search for places where these elements are plentiful.

⭐ Types of Map: Weather Maps

FACTS

Weather maps show the weather of an area for a particular period of time. They can show weather and temperature predictions, such as sunshine or rainfall. Some weather maps forecast the weather of a large area, such as a country or continent. Weather maps are important for travelers and pilots to know the weather of where they are and where they are going.

Study this weather map showing the highest temperature forecast (in °F) for many cities in the United States in the month of August in 2015. Then answer the questions below.

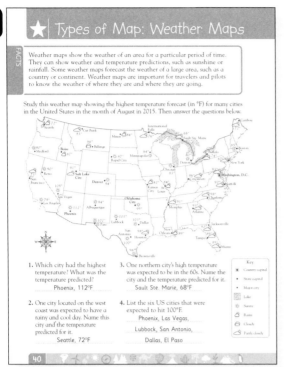

1. Which city had the highest temperature? What was the temperature predicted?
Phoenix, 112°F

2. One city located on the west coast was expected to have a rainy and cool day. Name this city and the temperature predicted for it.
Seattle, 72°F

3. One northern city's high temperature was expected to be in the 60s. Name the city and the temperature predicted for it.
Sault Ste. Marie, 68°F

4. List the six US cities that were expected to hit 100°F.
Phoenix, Las Vegas, Lubbock, San Antonio, Dallas, El Paso

Key
- Country capital
- State capital
- Major city
- Lake
- Sunny
- Rainy
- Cloudy
- Partly cloudy

Weather maps make it easy for travelers to see weather predictions across a wide area. Ask your child, "Would it be better or worse if this information were presented as a list with words and numbers?" Then discuss the reasons for his or her answer.

United States: Physical Features ⭐

FACTS

The United States of America is the third-largest country in the world. It has varied natural features, such as the fertile Great Plains, the five Great Lakes, and the Rocky Mountains. The country also has many dry and sandy deserts, green valleys, and dense swamps.

Study this physical map of the United States and then circle the correct answer below.

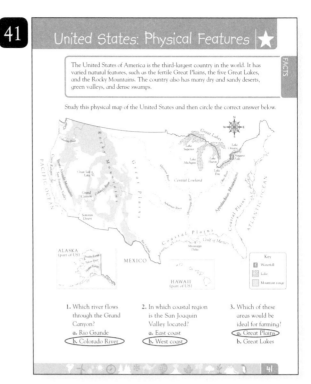

Key
- Waterfall
- Lake
- Mountain range

1. Which river flows through the Grand Canyon?
a. Rio Grande
b. Colorado River ✓

2. In which coastal region is the San Joaquin Valley located?
a. East coast
b. West coast ✓

3. Which of these areas would be ideal for farming?
a. Great Plains ✓
b. Great Lakes

This map of the US shows its physical features. Ask: "Which half of the US is the most mountainous?" and "Are there any mountains in the other half?" Ask your child to show you an area that has no mountains.

⭐ United States: Political Divisions

FACTS

The capital of the United States of America is Washington, D.C. It is where the branches of the US government are located. In addition to the national capital, all 50 US states have their own capital cities, too. These state capitals are cities in which state governments make their laws and regulations.

This map shows the capital cities of the 48 contiguous or connected states in the US. Use this map to write the capital cities for the states listed below.

State Name	Capital City
Texas	Austin
North Dakota	Bismarck
Wisconsin	Madison
Nevada	Carson City
Maine	Augusta

Key
- Country capital
- State capital
- Lake

Ask your child to name the capital of the state where you live. Talk about your state's government and some issues that it handles. Together, go online and find a photo of the capitol building. Then explain that it is the place where lawmakers meet.

United States: Alaska and Hawaii ⭐

FACTS

In 1959, Alaska and Hawaii became the 49th and 50th states of the US. These two are the only US states that are not connected to the US mainland. Alaska is the largest US state and has very cold winters because of its location near the Arctic Circle. In contrast, Hawaii is a series of small islands in the Pacific Ocean. It has a warm climate all year round.

Study these maps of Alaska and Hawaii. Using these maps and information from above, write down three similarities and three differences between these states.
Note: The first one has been done for you.

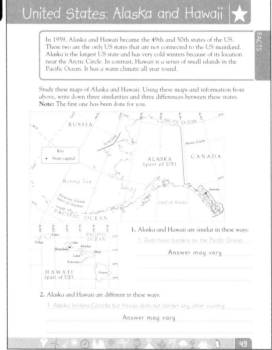

Key
- State capital

1. Alaska and Hawaii are similar in these ways:
1. Both have borders on the Pacific Ocean
Answer may vary

2. Alaska and Hawaii are different in these ways:
1. Alaska borders Canada but Hawaii does not border any other country
Answer may vary

This page points out two key contrasts—climate and size—between Alaska and Hawaii. Look for more details about the two states and see if you and your child can list other ways in which Alaska and Hawaii differ.

★ United States: Historical Maps

Maps can show us the difference between the world as it was years ago and the world as it is today. Ancient maps show what people thought the world looked like hundreds of years ago. These ancient maps changed as explorers discovered unknown lands and new information was added to these maps to make them more accurate. The latest maps show all the countries and cities that are known. Comparing these maps can reveal what has changed over time.

The maps on the facing page show the east coast of the United States. The first map shows the 13 British colonies in 1775, just before the American Revolutionary War. The second map shows the east coast of the United States as it is today. Study the maps and then answer the questions below.

1. The state of New Hampshire was larger in 1775 than it is today. Which state was later carved out from New Hampshire to make a new state?

Vermont

2. In the map of 1775, the northernmost colony belonged to Massachusetts. It later became a new state. What is the name of that state?

Maine

3. The area under West Florida is now part of the states of Alabama and Mississippi. Find two more differences between the map of 1775 map and today's map. Write them below.

Answer may vary

Maps tell us where things are with up-to-date information. But, as these two pages show, maps can also be snapshots of the past. On the US map of 1775, point out where "Province of Quebec" was, and talk about what that area is today.

United States: Historical Maps ★

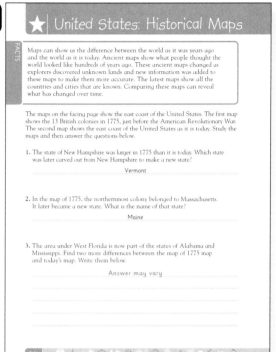

4. Name the seven colonies on the map of 1775 that have similar borders to that of the states as they are drawn in today's US map.

South Carolina,
Maryland,
Delaware,
New Jersey,
Connecticut,
Rhode Island,
Massachusetts

The historic map labels "Spain" as holding land beyond the Mississippi, and "Indian Reserve" in parts of today's Tennessee, Georgia, and Alabama. This page offers you an opportunity to begin relating the complex story of how the US grew through conquest, purchase, and negotiations.

★ United States: Time Zones

As the Earth rotates, half of it points toward the sun and the other half points away. In some parts of the world, it is daytime, while in other it is nighttime. Time zones were created to know the time in different places around the world. The US crosses six time zones, four of which are in mainland US. So, when it is 9 AM in the Eastern Time Zone, it will be 8 AM in the Central Time Zone, 7 AM in the Mountain Time Zone, and 6 AM in the Pacific Time Zone. As for the other two states, it will be 5 AM in most of Alaska—the part that is in the Alaskan Time Zone. At the same moment, in standard time, it will be 4 AM in Hawaii, which is located in the Hawaii-Aleutian Time Zone.

This map shows the time zones in the US. Imagine that you are in Columbia, South Carolina, and need to call friends in other cities. If it is 3 PM in Columbia, write what time it will be in the cities listed below.

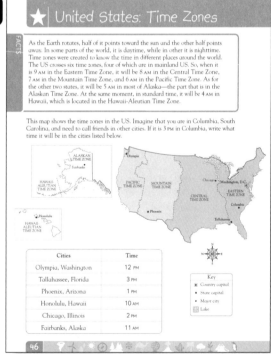

Cities	Time
Olympia, Washington	12 PM
Tallahassee, Florida	3 PM
Phoenix, Arizona	1 PM
Honolulu, Hawaii	10 AM
Chicago, Illinois	2 PM
Fairbanks, Alaska	11 AM

Until the 1880s, time zones did not exist: every place estimated its own time from the sun's position. This was a problem for train schedules! Help your child explore this surprising history by reading a children's book on the subject, such as *Time Zones* by David A. Adler.

Geography and Earth's Future ★

We live on a beautiful planet. It is filled with many natural features and a variety of plants and animals. However, there are many things that pose a danger to the Earth and its future. It is up to us, the people of Earth, to work together and find ways to protect our planet.

We can protect the Earth in many ways. Take a look at the sentences below about saving the Earth's resources. Use words from the word box to complete them.

Bag	Donate
Clean	Pollution
Paper	Electricity

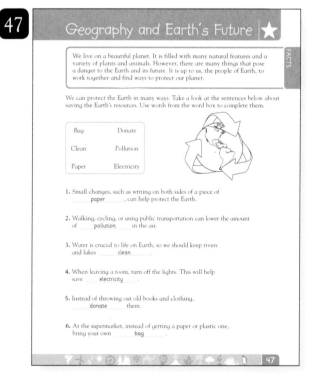

1. Small changes, such as writing on both sides of a piece of _____ paper _____, can help protect the Earth.

2. Walking, cycling, or using public transportation can lower the amount of _____ pollution _____ in the air.

3. Water is crucial to life on Earth, so we should keep rivers and lakes _____ clean _____.

4. When leaving a room, turn off the lights. This will help save _____ electricity _____.

5. Instead of throwing out old books and clothing, _____ donate _____ them.

6. At the supermarket, instead of getting a paper or plastic one, bring your own _____ bag _____.

The activity on this page gives children ideas about things they can do to help the Earth, such as reduce wastage and pollution. Together come up with more ways to protect Earth. Then ask your child, "Which of these ideas do you want to try?"